Graduating from Church School

Maturing in Christ

Franklin L Cunningham

Cunningham Enterprises
Published by Cunningham Enterprises
Charlotte, North Carolina U.S.A
www.francbillions.com

Copyright © 2013 by Franklin L. Cunningham
All rights reserved.

Cunningham, Franklin L.
Graduating from Church School / Franklin L. Cunningham

ISBN: 978-0-615-83657-7

Printed in the United States of America

Cover Design & Layout by Jessica Hammer
www.sorcadesign.com

Photo by Sydney K. Cunningham
neinei011.wix.com/sydneyzoominphotos

Without limiting the rights under copyright reserved above, no part of this publication may be reproduced, stored in or introduced into a retrieval system, or transmitted, in any form, or by any means (electronic, mechanical, photocopying, recording, or otherwise), without written permission of the publisher of this book.

The scanning, uploading, and distribution of this book via the Internet or via any other means without the permission of the publisher is illegal and punishable by law.
Please purchase only authorized electronic editions, and do not participate in or encourage electronic piracy of copyright materials. Your support of the author's rights is appreciated.

Unless otherwise indicated, all Scriptures quotations are from the King James Version of the Bible, © 1988 by the B.B. Kirkbride Bible Company, Inc. The Thompson Chain – Reference Bible Improved Edition by Frank Charles Thompson.
http://www.kingjamesbibleonline.org

Word definitions marked WAD are from Webster's American Dictionary College Edition, © 1997 by Random House, Inc.

Word definitions marked UBD are from Unger's Bible Dictionary, © 1957, 1961, 1966 by Moody Bible Institute of Chicago, Third Edition.

Quotes marked KJV are from the King James Version of the Bible.
Quotes marked SOF are original works from the Songs of Franklin.

Kingdom of God University

Charlotte, North Carolina

Having completed the Course of Study and fulfilled all requirements, the Faculty and the Board of Trustees hereby award

Franklin Lamar Cunningham

with the degree of

Deacon of Christ

He is entitled to all the rights, honors, privileges, and responsibilities of that degree.

Given on this ninth day of August, two thousand and six.

∧

God the Son
Chairman of the Board of Trustees

God the Father
President of the University

God the Holy Spirit
Vice-President for Academic Affairs

Table of Contents

Part 1

Chapter 1	13
Chapter 2	21
Chapter 3	29
Chapter 4	37

Part 2

Chapter 6	59
Chapter 7	75
Chapter 8	87
Chapter 9	93

Part 3

Chapter 10	113
Chapter 11	121
Chapter 12	127
Chapter 13	135

Appreciation

To Felice Gerwitz and Viktorija Girton, I give special thanks for believing in me and helping edit this book. I am truly grateful. Thank you for trusting the Lord God and walking after the Spirit.

About the Author

Franklin L. Cunningham is a husband, and the father of two daughters. He has a B.A. degree in Industrial Management and is a mortgage loan professional for over twenty-two years. Franklin lives in North Carolina and is currently teaching a financial literacy curriculum at a correctional center for men. His credo is, "Don't take it lightly that God has made you a man!" Franklin mission is to inspire God's people to establish a Godly financial mindset.

This book is dedicated to the Lord God.

May it help God's people become believers.

GRADUATING FROM CHURCH SCHOOL

Part 1

1

"Holy Spirit?"

"Yes, Franklin."

"How much longer must I deal with this?"

"Deal with what, Franklin?"

"Church school."

"Who told you that you had to go to church school?"

"My parents, grandparents, and pastors."

"Why?"

"They said to learn about God."

"Are you talking about the Lord God?"

"Yes."

"Well Franklin, did you learn about the Lord God?"

"I heard about God from my parents, grandparents and pastors. The pastors preached and hollered, a lot. I learned about God by studying the Word for myself.

"Franklin, who opened your heart with a hunger to learn?"

"You, Lord, You!"

This is a message for all ages: "I write unto you, little children, because your sins are forgiven you for his name's sake. I write unto you, fathers, because ye have known him that is from the beginning. I write unto you, young men, because ye have overcome the wicked one." (1 John 2:12-13)

When I was a child, I acted like a child. When I was a young son, I acted like a young son. Now that I am a father, I act like one. Simply put, graduating from church school means maturing past the elementary things of this world and becoming a new creation in Christ. I never heard anyone say that people are not supposed to go to a church building their entire lives. Therefore, I went. I listened to my pastors and I learned from their teachings. I didn't rely on the Holy Spirit. No, I followed men and what they said. This essentially held me back from all that the Lord had for me to learn and to share with others.

Now as a believer in Christ, led by the Holy Spirit, I feel that while church has a purpose, especially for the young Christian believer, there is a bigger purpose that the Lord has for those who want to go beyond the elementary teachings. Truly, God's call is for each and every one of us. And the only way that I know how to share this with you is for you to pray and seek the Lord before you read every chapter of this book.

It is not I, Franklin, who wants to convict you of truth. If I did, this would be just another book. Here, within the pages you hold in your hand, even if it is in a digital format, you are being instructed and challenged to listen to the voice of the Holy Spirit and what He instructs. In this book, I want to challenge you to listen to the Holy Spirit in a new way. Some of you may not have that deep of a relationship with God that you will hear His voice. The challenge for you is to keep at it every day. Practice, give God some time, and expect miracles!

I eventually did. I grew up and began to trust the Holy Spirit. In this way, I am a graduate from church school and I work for the kingdom of God. With the help of the Holy Spirit, I have learned that, "Not forsaking the assembling of ourselves together…." (Heb. 10:25) does not mean that the only way I can assemble with other believers is go to the church building. I can still assemble and praise the Lord. But if I chose to attend church, it is because of love, not obligation, that I do so.

As a child, I remember attending church almost every Sunday. At times, I had some fun. Too much fun! I attended a family church, so most of the members were made up of friends and family. I enjoyed going because I was able to run and play with my relatives after the service.

We could not sit together during the church service because we would get in trouble for talking. Many Sundays, my brother and I were punished for talking or hitting each other. As soon as the pastor gave the benediction, we bolted outside as fast as our legs could take us.

One time, my mother had to sit in front of my brother and me because there was not enough room in the pew for the three of us.

My brother and I took advantage of this opportunity to misbehave, unaware that our dad had slipped into the pew behind us.

As soon as we started whispering and pushing each other, whomp! My dad thumped my brother hard on the back of the head. I started laughing and whomp! My father then thumped me on the head. That was the end of the fun and we did not try it again. Lesson learned.

Nevertheless, I found it difficult as a young person to sit through the service and pay attention for three hours, staying silent and still. Sitting on those hard wooden pews, not a cushion in sight, was no help either. It was a relief when everyone was asked to stand for the reading and singing of the hymns because otherwise, my legs would go numb from sitting there.

However, my legs would get equally tired of standing because we sang so many hymns. The deacons would sing these hymns called "long meters" that seemed to last forever.

I began to get creative in order to make it through the services. I drew, wrote, hummed, and at times, even fell asleep. This wasn't effective. I tried to learn the hymns, but only certain people sang certain songs at specific times. In addition, the same songs were not sung every Sunday, which made it difficult to learn a hymn. I did manage to learn one hymn, but only because of how the deacon sang the song.

One of my favorite hymns was "Until I Die," but my entire childhood I thought the song was "Un Tell I Die" because that is what deacon was saying.

It went a little something like this:

"Un tell I die – die – die
Un tell I die – die – die
I'm gonna serve God any how
Tell I die."

This was the song that got me through many Sunday services. My brother and I mimicked it our entire childhood. I would sing "Un tell I die" silently in my mind and whenever the deacon got the opportunity to sing it during a service, so did I. It was my golden opportunity to out sing him and I would, at the top of my voice. "UN TELL I DIE – DIE – DIE!!!" Just like him. Even now, I am thankful to that deacon for the fuel to stay awake and out of trouble during services.

At every service, I would pester my mother to let me sit with my cousins. The answer was always the same. "No!" I figured out that the only way I could sit with them was if I was part of the children's choir. The problem with that option was that we had to sit on the same platform as the pastor and we faced the congregation. All eyes would be on the choir stand.

I knew my parents did not really trust my brother and me to sit together in front of the congregation due to our previous bad behavior. Yet we received the opportunity to redeem ourselves. After we joined the children's choir, it seemed as though every time I looked out into the congregation, my mother was staring right at me, saying with her eyes that I better not embarrass her. And I didn't.

The other things I enjoyed about church were the holiday seasons. I have memories of the treats we would receive, the dinners, the plays, singing in the children's choir, and receiving those brown paper bags containing an orange, apple, peppermint candy cane, and a couple of walnuts or pecans.

Another good thing about the church was its proximity from our home. We only lived a few minutes away and my mom, aunt, and both of my grandmothers would prepare Sunday's dinner on Saturday night. This way, we could eat as soon as we returned home from church. That was the best.

One thing that I did not like was the Sundays the pastor would stop by my grandmother's house for dinner. The children would have to wait outside until he and his wife were finished, then we were allowed in to eat.

I have to admit, my ten-year-old self used to call the pastor and his wife greedy people. After all, we were hungry kids that were made to stand outside. And it felt like forever; we thought they would never leave. I was even upset with my grandmother because she gave them the best pieces of the chicken: the legs. Hot-toe-mighty! I was so upset because they never invited my grandparents to their house to eat. I promised myself that when I was married, my wife would never be required to feed the pastor's family.

Unfortunately, I do not remember learning much about the Scriptures while attending church as a youngster because I only recall the pastors preaching to us; not teaching the doctrines of Christ. I also don't remember much Scripture teaching happening at home either. Although I would read the Bible on my own from time to time, I was not consistent. So I did not remember what I read.

I do remember my grandmothers, Corrie Bell and Geneva, praying out loud at nighttime before they went to bed. My grandmother Geneva would call out everyone's name individually while she prayed for them. She spent so long praying that I sometimes fell asleep listening to her. She covered my brother Donnie and me with her prayers.

As far as I can remember, I have always believed there was a God. I was reminded of that every time I went outside and looked at nature. I grew up in the country and I loved being outside all day long. Those were the good ole days, but at some point, I had to graduate and grow up, and I did. In this book, I will share the process of my spiritual growth in the hopes that the Holy Spirit touches you and that you grow into a deeper relationship with our Lord. He is waiting.

I was born from an alabaster box
So, Jesus' feet I washed a lot.
I'm on the top and I'm hot,
I'm like a fiery furnace
That wouldn't burn up
Because the presence of Jesus I've felt
You better buckle up your belt.
In parables, I speak.
Anointed by the fire of the Spirit.
Because the Master has given merit to it,
Eternal fire is bearable as He sees fit.
It doesn't exist in time, and it isn't a variable,
It's going to take you awhile and prayer to figure out this parable.
Because sadness invades your heart,
The world pulls you away from the Master and it's easy to part.
Can you hear me as I speak to you spiritually?
Possibly not because you're entrenched in worldly pursuit.

Worldly minded like many who preach.
It is time to call on the Master to teach.
Time to stop being a church actor or actress,
As many sit in the pews devoid of real faith.
A hollowness pervading their hearts that is difficult to fake.
In that way it is challenging to hear from the Holy Spirit—
It is time to study to show yourself approved!
And become a graduate from church school.

  Songs of Franklin (SOF)

2

Father, I thank you for your love and grace. For you loved us so much that you gave us your only begotten son. Father, I pray that this book will help express to others how much you really love us, not how much we love you. Lord God, I thank you for giving me big faith. Holy Spirit, please help us to have big faith in the Lord's love for us.

Graduation indicates advancement to a higher rank or degree. Graduating from church school showed that I matured in Christ: I studied to show myself approved and passed whatever tests the Lord God set before me. Moreover, I now apply the Word of God to my daily life and trust the Holy Spirit to lead, guide, and direct me. The Lord God wants me to follow the Spirit and not the things of the flesh. This means I need to line up my life behind the Holy Spirit and let him lead me.

Through study and prayer, I have interpreted this to mean that I'm not obligated to follow the lightweight formalism of the religious law, such as paying tithes of mint, anise, and cumin. True religion is focusing on the weightier matters of religious law, such as judgment, mercy, and faith. If my focus remains on these things, at least my mind is on the things of the Spirit and not the things of this world.

Think about it this way: if I'm focusing on judgment, mercy, and faith, then my mind is on God the Father (judgment), God the Son (mercy), and God the Holy Spirit (faith). Before attending church school, I had found myself focusing on religion and the things of this world.

Read the verse below and prayerfully consider the following version of the same verse:

"Therefore leaving the principles of the doctrine of Christ, let us go on unto perfection; not laying again the foundation of repentance from dead works, and of faith toward God, Of the doctrine of baptisms, and of laying on of hands, and of resurrection of the dead, and of eternal judgment. And this will we do, if God permits."
(Heb. 6:1-3)

Amplified version: "Therefore let us go on and get past the ELEMENTARY stage in the teaching and doctrine of Christ [the Messiah], advancing steadily toward the completeness and perfection that belong to Spiritual maturity. Let us not again be laying the foundation of repentance and abandonment of dead works [dead formalism] and of the faith [by which you turned] to God. With teachings about purifying, the laying on of hands, the resurrection from the dead, and eternal judgment and punishment. [These are all matters of which you should have been fully aware long, long, ago.] If indeed God permits, we will [now] proceed [to advance teaching]." (Heb. 6:1-3)

Graduating from church school cannot get any simpler than this. I now know that if I had not experienced the laying on of hands in the church I was attending, my spiritual life would be somewhere between that of a pre-kindergarten's and a fourth grader's. If I was anointed through the laying on of hands, I would have the equivalent of a fifth or sixth grader's spirituality. The Bible states the need to grow up spiritually. And this is what I was not doing.

I didn't go to church school because I felt I knew a little more than the pastor. It was as if I was in pre-kindergarten and the pastor was a pre-kindergarten preacher/teacher. In this scenario, I could only move to the next grade of kindergarten in a year, and there I would sit under yet another teacher of the primary grades. My faith was at a primary level. I needed more.

Some people have spiritually been in pre-kindergarten for years. In real school, you don't repeat the elementary grades over and over again. So why would you do this in the church? It is time for graduation. This was a revelation! It occurred to me that in my years of church attendance, I had been repeating the same spiritual grade, so to speak, year after year. This was unheard of in the world of education. I knew I needed to move on, but where was I to go? And the bigger question was, why was I still sitting there, learning nothing new, going unchallenged, and receiving no spiritual growth? It was at this pivotal point that I grabbed my proverbial crayons, coloring books, and fat pencil and high-tailed it out of that church! What was I thinking? I did not know.

I only knew with a certainty that comes from the Holy Spirit that I could do better by studying with the Lord. I knew he was calling me to a deeper spiritual level and I struggled in my decision to leave the church, as it went against everything I had been taught.

While in church school, I should have been studying in the same way a person studies in grade school. But I wasn't. I was failing most of the spiritual tests the Lord put before me. I wasn't studying and I wasn't being challenged by the pastors to improve. It should have not taken me sixteen years to graduate from church school.

It took Christ three and a half years to teach the disciples how to live a godly life. Today, it is taking people a lifetime to learn this three and a half year process. Most fall short. Many carnal minded or worldly men attempt to teach a spiritual gospel and they cannot. I made a decision not to put my trust in a man. While a preacher can spend hours teaching about the Word of God, it is up to the Holy Spirit to convict. Is your heart open to conviction? Mine wasn't. It was as if I sat there, blind and deaf. I saw and I heard, but the message fell on blind eyes and deaf ears. Only the Holy Spirit can teach spiritual living.

It is the day of the Lord: we must help God's people to become believers in Christ Jesus. Let me say that this is not some narcissistic exercise in self-aggrandizement. "Whom the son set free is free indeed." (Jn. 8:36) Praise the Lord from whom all blessings flow. One day, my wife sent me a text that said, "Oh Thou of Big Faith!!!" It spoke to me. You see, love gives and faith means taking that step and giving back. I take as much as the Lord God has to give me. To me, oh thou of little faith translate to mean that you take too little. Why do you take so little from the Lord who has vast amounts to give? Do you not know that every time you take from him he replenishes? He is a font of mercy and a well of outpouring grace!

The Bible speaks of the woman with the issue of blood (Mt. 9:20). She had faith that Christ Jesus heals. So, in faith, she accepted and touched his hem, only wanting a little of the abundance he had to offer. In this case, her faith overruled obedience. She had obeyed the law for over twelve years. It was against the law for her to be out in public. She knew if she continued to be obedient to the law, she would miss this divine encounter. Her faith took over and overruled the opinion of others. She stepped out in trust and was immediately healed. Hallelujah in the name of Christ Jesus!

Her faith healed her. She graduated from obedience to faith.

Not only did the woman's faith heal her, it allowed for a personal experience with God the Son and she saw his face. Moses never had the same opportunity to see the face of God the Father. He was under the law. Being under the old covenant law meant he was not given the opportunity, since old covenant law dictated that man was to follow behind God. But when the woman of faith in the New Testament reached out to touch the hem of Jesus, the Son of the living God, he turned around and showed her his face. In essence, she was seeing the face of love, healing, and mercy. He, in turn, saw her faith. What a revelation! I pray that you too will seek the faith that requires you to take chances, to reach out, touch the hem of our Lord, and believe! This is having a big faith in the Lord God.

The example of the woman's story is not a license to break the law. It is an example of the Lord changing the old covenant into the new covenant. We know that the old covenant had its purpose. But in sending Christ the Redeemer, the Lord had bigger things in store for us. This lady of faith took a monumental step that has been recorded in the Holy Scriptures for us to read and to ponder.

In the New Testament, we read about the leper who also broke the old covenant law by making a public appearance after he was healed by Christ Jesus (Mark 1:40-45). The leper's faith was so strong that he risked death in order to have life. It was his faith that healed him.

Jesus put out his hand, touched the leper, and healed him. The leper was then instructed not to say anything to any man. But as soon as this believer broke away from Jesus, he blazed a trail, publically giving witness about what Jesus had done for him. He could not help telling everyone.

Blind Bartemaeus broke the law when he refused to be quiet after he learned that Jesus of Nazareth, the Son of David, was in his presence (Mark 10:46-52). He took advantage of his opportunity and was immediately healed. Many of the people during that time tried to keep Bartemaeus quiet, but this caused him to shout louder. His need to be healed overpowered his fear. Bartemaeus' faith healed him.

Whenever you have an important opportunity or importunity to be healed of infirmities by the love of God, step out in faith and be healed. Not everyone with faith is healed and we all are witnesses to that. However, God always hears our prayers. He heals us when he is ready, in his perfect time.

The blind man (Mark 10:46-52) sat at the gate for years. Jesus must have passed him by multiple times without healing him. But when the time was right, the man cried out and the Lord heard and healed him. Our faith and love for him must be unshakable. Love transcends any illness we may have.

Several years ago, I broke an Old Testament law. I had always thought I would be cursed if I did not tithe exactly ten percent of my income to a specific church as the pastor instructed each Sunday. My church preachers constantly hammered home this lesson and I was fearful. I paid a tithe not out of love for God, but out of obligation. Through prayer, I received the revelation that Christ was covering my finances; I was blessed whether or not I tithed ten percent to the church. Instead, my tithe could go towards helping another brother or sister in the Lord or it could be a love offering at church. And if God so instructed, I could even give more than ten percent.

This was such a revelation to me! I was blessed. I listened to the Holy Spirit. Immediately, I was healed of the fear, sense of duty, and obligation I had previously felt and I began prospering in every area of my life. I realized if the Holy Spirit led me, I was to follow. My faith healed me.

Not only did I refocus my faith in Christ, I began to regain control of myself, both spiritually and financially. With the help of the Holy Spirit, I was inspired to write and publish my first book, Tithing: You Don't Have to Pay to Give. Tithing ten percent was not a magic formula to spiritual success. The Lord does not work like this.

Who do you know that is disconnected from Christ Jesus? Point them to the Word of God so that they can graduate from obedience to faith. Faith only comes one way: by hearing the Word of God.

"A wise man will hear, and will increase learning; and a man of understanding shall attain unto wise counsels...." (Prov. 1:5)

3

"In the beginning was the Word and the Word was with God, and the Word was God. The same was in the beginning with God." (John 1:1-2)

As with any study, there is a beginning, and for all Christians and true biblical scholars, it begins with the book of Genesis. Even the Gospel of John points to Genesis, and the beginning, in the wonderful verse above. Jesus was with God at the beginning of time. God the Father, God the Son, and God the Holy Spirit all existed outside of time and place.

Before the beginning of the world, God existed. God created the sun, moons, planets, and stars and set them in motion. In the beginning, the church was not yet a concept. God created all of the nationalities, races, creeds, and colors from our first parents, who were created in his own image. He then commanded them to replenish the earth. At this time, there was no formalized church.

These people were citizens of the kingdom. God spoke them into existence. Almighty God created "ex nihilo," Latin for "out of nothing." The Word is powerful. The Word can create. Life and death can be controlled by the power of the tongue.

We are challenged to understand the might of the tongue and are instructed to use it for good. In this way, we can praise God with our tongues, our voices, and our beings to worship him who gave us life.

In the following verses, you will find a wealth of information and insight into the ways of the Lord. It is time to delve deeper into his words. Read these verses here and then again in your own Bible. Be sure to keep a journal of your thoughts as you read these Scripture texts.

"The fear of the Lord is the beginning of knowledge: but fools despise wisdom and instruction." (Prov. 1:7)

"Grace and peace be multiplied unto you through the knowledge of God, and of Jesus our Lord...." (2 Pet. 1:2)

I challenge you to mature in Christ through wisdom and understanding. God's word is not meant to be hard. As a matter of fact, it is simple. God the Father has written it simply because he is preparing us to receive his Son, Jesus Christ. Begin to "study to shew thyself approved unto God, a workman that needeth not to be ashamed, rightly dividing the word of truth." (2 Tim. 2:15)

I know some people try to make the Bible out to be complex and unattainable. The Holy Spirit will enlighten your mind if you ask him. The word "revelation" means to reveal. The Lord God wants to reveal himself to you. I promise that if you read the Bible slowly and meditate on his Word, the Glory of the Lord will be revealed to you.

"For our rejoicing is this, the testimony of our conscience, that in simplicity and godly sincerity, not with fleshly wisdom, but by the grace of God, we have had our conversation in the world, and more abundantly to you-ward." (2 Cor. 1:12)

The Lord God said that he will teach us all things; we do not need a man to teach us everything. In the Old Testament, there was a hierarchy of teachers: the prophets and the scribes. These were the men who heard from God and proclaimed his message for the world. Still, man disobeyed. And when the people disobeyed, they were judged. We see this throughout salvation history. Yet God still loved us and the Father created a covenant with Abraham and Moses and then fulfilled that covenant in Christ.

Jesus came as a fulfillment of Isaiah's prophecy and continued this new covenant with man. By his death and resurrection, he opened the gates of heaven and offered man salvation. He chose disciples to spread the Word to all nations—before the Word was written, it traveled from place to place through those believers. Jesus wants the Body of Christ to come together—and he teaches us that where two or more are gathered in his name, he is in their midst.

People are tormented by a hope that will never come because they do not believe what the Holy Spirit is trying to tell them. Just like those people who were led by the prophets, and even those who followed Jesus, some just could not believe.

Sometimes people hope in their church leaders without taking the time to pray themselves. Other times, they receive a word from the Lord. In this case, it is considered a "private revelation," and must line up with Scripture. Our Bible is the test to which all revelations must conform.

Otherwise, man can come up with some crazy ideas that are not from the Lord at all! One of the reasons church hierarchy is so important is we have leaders who are ordained by God. Their teachings must line up with God's Word. But you will not know this until you take the time to study the Word of God. Then you may walk in faith, instead of hope.

Ideally, we are supposed to be walking by faith. Being guided only by hope is like driving 80 mph in a 65 mph zone and trusting that you will not get caught by the police. Whereas faith is driving the correct speed limit and knowing you will not get pulled over by the police.

Maturing in Christ means so many things. It is understanding that we can't serve two masters, or in essence, have "two" faces. It is truly a sin against God if we do. Prayerfully consider the verses below.

Two Faces—A Sin Against God

God doesn't like two faces.

You have to choose sides to run this race.

Which side do you choose?

Is it the good side, the bad side, or are you confused and can't decide? Well, either you're for Him or you're against Him.

Either you love Him or you hate Him.

There is no straddling the fence, no matter how high,

Because that high in God's eyes means bye-bye.

So don't cry! If you can't make up your mind,

Ungrateful soldier, get to the back of the line.

God needs soldiers that are not limited.

You can't experience His power being timid.

I hope you know that the devil is a set-up.

Oh, you didn't know he was a set-up, man? Shut up!

God's word is sufficient, my friend.

Take it for what it is, because He ain't going to bend.

If you put your hands in His hands, He'll do the rest, man.

Oh, I see the unconvinced is still not convinced.
Well, let me see if this makes sense.
There's only two sides, there is no lukewarm.
When you're lukewarm, either side can put one into your dome.
Because they don't really know what side you're on.
So, let your soul cry out.
He will hear you without a doubt.
Weeping may endure for a night,
But joy will surely come in the morn!
Believe me, the Word is born.

Never have I seen the righteous forsaken.
All of your tears will be taken.
God understand your tears, and at the faintest cry, He hears.
How will you know if God can bring you through?
Without trials?
Don't be in denial.
He knows how much you can bear.
You don't have to look up in the air.
All you have to do is stand.
And when you can't say a word, just wave your hands.

Don't you know that God has His eyes,
On Daniel, Pharaoh, and the sparrow?
What make you think that He is not watching you, yo?
Open your eyes and see the sun rise.
Are you surprised that every single thing dies?
No matter how hard life tries…
But I'm going to live forever!
It's what my heart says,
My hard head thinks otherwise—learning things the hard way.
It's not easy when the world keeps provoking me,
Especially when my ego keeps stroking me.
Each and every day I pray,
That the Lord takes this pain away.
So what, if I have to walk through this valley of the shadow of death! You think I'm doing this for my health?
I know the wages of sin is death.

And since I don't know how much of my time is left,
You pray for me and I'll pray for you.

In God's eyes, there is no time.
So when He is ready, I better be too,
And in faith, I claim heaven with you!

Song of Franklin (SOF)

Remembering the Past

When I was in seventh grade, there was a guy in my homeroom class that was huge. This kid was twice as big as everyone else in the class. He looked as though he should have been in high school. I thought to myself, this kid must be incapable of learning, otherwise why was he still in the seventh grade? We called him Big Tex because he told us that he was from Texas. Big Tex looked so out of place sitting in that seventh grade classroom. Later, I learned that he was not from Texas. He was actually from South Carolina and had grown up not too far from the school. Nevertheless, we continued calling him Big Tex.

After being in class with Big Tex for a week or so, I realized that he was not in the seventh grade because he could not learn; he was still there because he did not apply himself. He did not pay attention to the teacher; he did not take notes; he did not read; he did not study; and he did not do his class work or homework. He just showed up to school every day and sat there, picking on the kids that sat close to him. Every day, Big Tex came in one way and left the same way.

I found out that he was supposed to be in the ninth grade and was repeating the seventh grade for the third time. I wondered how anyone could fail the same grade twice. It was at this point that I made up my mind to never be like Big Tex. The only way that he could graduate to the next grade was if the teacher just passed him, even though he didn't do any of his work. Big Tex felt as though he already knew everything. And sure enough, after three years of being in the same grade, he finally moved to the eighth grade. The teacher didn't want him in the class anymore.

There are a lot of churchgoers like Big Tex. They are sitting in primary, grammar, elementary, middle, or high school church, repeating the same grade for three or more years when they should have graduated to the next level years ago. The problem is that they, like Big Tex, did not learn the lessons or did not care about maturing in their spiritual life. Take Big Tex's story as a warning.

"At that time Jesus answered and said, I thank thee, O Father, Lord of heaven and earth, because thou hast hid these things from the wise and prudent, and hast revealed them unto babes." (Matt. 11:25)

The truth is simple: the love of God is for all. But it takes our participation. We can sit in one place, taking no action, or we can open our eyes and our hearts to the truth that the Word of God reveals to "babes." I pray to the Holy Spirit as I am writing this book that you are encouraged to seek Christ in a deeper way. More than likely, you are not as far along spiritually as you should be. This book is designed to elevate your thinking. I urge you to come up to a higher grade; graduate from where you are and increase your faith in God.

4

Holy Spirit, I pray that you encourage the person reading this book to study the Word of God chapter by chapter, verse by verse. Help him or her to understand the things of the Spirit and to trust in you. Amen.

On average, I believe that many pastors stand in their pulpits and unknowingly, preach a twisted version of God's word. If you do not know the Lord God's Word for yourself, you will be deceived. Do you know the difference between the truth and a lie? Are you being deceived? Pulpits are filled with people who go through the motions out of obligation. You may be a sincere believer—but are you growing in knowledge and faith? Are you being challenged?

The Lord God will motivate you to grow when it is time for

you to graduate. When the Holy Spirit starts speaking to you, it is a good time for you to check your motivation. He will nudge your spirit if you are in tune with Him. Most people do not realize what that means.

Spiritual unrest has to do with wanting to learn more, but leaving church unfed and spiritually hungry. In such a case, you should go home, take out the Bible, and see if there is an additional study you can do based upon the pastor's teachings. Get into the Word of God. Don't expect to be completely fed in church.

For years, my body sat in church, but my spirit was missing. My spirit and the Holy Spirit were in two completely different realms. Then one day, I was in prayer and I felt as if my spirit had left the building with the Lord. When the spirit returned to my body, it was time to go home. The first time this happened to me, I remained aware of what was going on during the church service, but I was more in tune to what the Holy Spirit was saying to me while I was reading Scripture or praying.

For those of you who may be new to revelation, it is a time when you hear or understand a deeper truth in your heart (your spirit). Sometimes the Holy Spirit may talk to you directly while you are in prayer or in the middle of reading God's Word. It is prudent to write down what is being revealed and to measure it against the Scriptures. God will never reveal anything harmful or negative. If the message sounds bad, it is probably from the enemy. Private revelation is a personal way to grow in faith. It can lead you into a deeper conversation with God, teach you a specific truth, or even answer a question you have. It does not add or detract from Scripture. It is just for you.

If you are new to revelation, it would be wise for a spiritually mature person to help you discern whether or not the revelation is from the Lord. A spiritual advisor can help us grow in the Lord. Some pastors are really good at revelations and have training in this area.

In my case, the Lord began revealing through different signs that I was ready to graduate from church school. At the time, I did not realize these signs implied graduation. I was not paying attention to what was going on during the service. The praise and worship leader had everyone standing up and clapping their hands. I couldn't participate. I was enthralled in what I was reading in my Bible and I began writing down what the Holy Spirit was revealing to me through the book of Revelation. I was reading about what the Lord God liked and disliked about his seven churches.

Soon, the singing ended and the pastor began preaching about the three Hebrew boys in the fiery furnace. But I didn't hear anything he said. I was immersed in the Word--reading chapters one, two, and three of Revelation.

The Lord spoke to me in the following verses:

"…Fear not; I am the first and the last: I am he that liveth, and was dead; and, behold, I am alive for evermore, Amen; and have the keys of hell and of death. Write the things which thou hast seen, and the things which are, and the things which shall be hereafter; The mystery of the seven stars which thou sawest in my right hand, and the seven golden candlesticks. The seven stars are the angels of the seven churches: and the seven candlesticks which thou sawest are the seven churches." (Rev. 1:17-20)

"I was in the Spirit on the Lord's day, and heard behind me a great voice, as of a trumpet, Saying, I am Alpha and Omega, the first and the last: and, What thou seest, write in a book, and send it unto the seven churches which are in Asia; unto Ephesus, and unto Smyrna, and unto Pergamos, and unto Thyatira, and unto Sardis, and unto Philadelphia, and unto Laodicea." (Rev. 1:10-11)

"[Father, I pray the Gospel for Asia.] Blessed is he that readeth, and they that hear the words of this prophecy, and keep those things which are written therein: for the time is at hand." (Rev. 1:3)

Another time, the Lord gave me a sign that I was ready to graduate by revealing something in a specific season. When I attended church, my pastor confirmed this first by reading a particular Scripture passage and secondly, by mentioning something that God had already revealed to me. I took this as a confirmation that the Lord was indeed speaking to me. I began to trust that it was truly the Holy Spirit within me.

On the one hand, I thought that if the Lord was giving me this information first hand, why should I continue going to church for confirmation? Let me just say, it is a gift from the Lord to receive confirmation. It is totally by his grace that he reveals truth to us. No matter what stage of your spiritual journey you're in, it is important that you realize this.

I was able to trust what the Lord was telling me by faith. It is the Holy Spirit's job to write God's laws, precepts, and commandments on my heart and to lead, guide, and direct me into all truth.

Don't get me wrong; confirmation is a good thing. It means we are on the right track. It keeps us humble. It's also important to remember that not all revelation is from God. Sometimes the evil one tries to emulate the Lord. We must put on the armor of Christ to ward off confusing thoughts and ideas (Eph. 6:11). As I stated earlier, having a spiritual advisor or prayer partner is important. If you are married, your spouse can be your prayer partner. It will help strengthen your marriage if you both pray together daily.

A pastor who can help you grow in the faith is one who understands private revelation and encourages a congregation to study the Word of God outside of church. Sometimes we can get so busy with committees and meetings that we forget the true focus of church. Church is a community where we worship God together publicly. It also helps us grow in our faith. If your church falls short of that, it may be time to find another.

Listening to the Holy Spirit takes practice and hard work. You must go to God in quiet and repent of wrong doings, then praise him for his sanctifying grace. Read a passage of Scripture slowly, allowing the words to sink into your heart. At times, the Word of God is a two-edged sword and God will correct and chastise us. Remember this: a walk with the Lord isn't without trial. If you forget, re-read the Song of Franklin in the previous chapter. I pray the Lord speaks to your heart and confirms his word to you!

> Welcome to the Carolinas,
> Nowhere is the Bible belt finer!
> Here we don't spare the rod,
> And boy, you better watch your step.
> Now it is time to learn these concepts,
> Before I flex my biceps.
> You should get to know the law and precepts.

> You know how that thing goes,
> If you don't know, then you better learn the lingo.
> Or find out real quick where my chains go.
> In case you didn't know,
> Ask the Holy Spirit,
> And He'll tell you so.
> Come on, John Doe,
> Ask the Holy Spirit.
> He's your guide,
> He'll never lie.
> For the Son, He came and for you He died.
> Songs of Franklin (SOF)

The word that came to me from the Lord instructed me to write everything that he had spoken to me privately and compile it into a book. Grace for grace had been given.

I look back now and see that I had indeed graduated from many church schools in my life. The first was my childhood church in South Carolina. I attended two small family churches. One of them, my father's parents attended, and the other, my family attended. I really liked the people at these two churches. They always made me feel right at home.

The church services were very similar. The order consisted of prayer, praise and worship, preaching, singing, and benediction. Both pastors preached and hollered a lot and had a hoop at the end of every sermon. A hoop is something that most Baptist preachers do towards the end of their sermons to let the congregation know that they are about to finish. The preacher reads one or two Scripture verses, goes off into Neverland with his message, and leaves me trying to remember what those Scripture verses were that he just read. In other words, the preacher goes way off-track.

The little real teaching that I did receive was in Sunday school, but it came from a Sunday school book which may have consisted of parallel verses that the pastor taught about, but was not directly from the Bible itself. We did not bring Bibles to class, this I remember. In addition, I cannot recall attending a Bible study at either church.

While a Sunday morning service would be the perfect place for the pastor to teach God's Word, that's not what usually happened. The pastor never asked us to get out our Bibles and follow along. As a matter of fact, my preachers stated that they had been called to preach, not to teach.

As an adult, this is confusing to me. The Bible states that it is foolish to preach to somebody about who God is when you can walk outside, look around, and see the glory of God's creation. What we were getting from our church didn't qualify as even the equivalent of a first grade spiritual education; it was more like a head start church school.

Now I realize why I was confused for so long. I could never share with anyone what the pastor had preached because his sermons weren't backed by Scripture. His teachings had no impact on me. I was like Big Tex to the tenth power. I was repeating the same grade, year after year, and never passing to the next grade. At least Big Tex eventually moved on to the next grade and was able to experience a higher level of teaching.

In the secular world, I had completed twelve years of public school. I was a student athlete in baseball, football, and basketball. I had graduated in the eighth percentile of my class. By the time I graduated high school; I had a stellar academic background and was actively being recruited by colleges. But on a spiritual level, I was still in kindergarten church school.

I am so glad that I had the opportunity to attend college. The university I attended was a private Baptist institution of higher learning in North Carolina. As such, it was based on Christian values.

The word "university" comes from the words "unit" and "diversity." Until I attended a church service in college, I thought that every church in the world was the same as the two churches I grew up attending. For the first time, I encountered a pastor who actually taught from the Bible and not a Sunday school book. I had never heard a preacher teach from the Bible. It was eye opening to me and at this point in my life; I started delving into the Scriptures for myself.

The more I read, the more I realized there was more to faith than just going to church on Sunday: sitting in a pew, singing, and paying tithes. I started to get convicted. I felt I still had not given my life to Christ. I had gone to the front of the church as a child and repeated Romans 10:9 to the pastor. I was baptized at a young age, but I did it out of formality, not because of a changed heart. You have to have a changed heart to receive Jesus as your Lord and Savior.

I believe there are millions of people who have gone to the front of the church and repeated Romans 10:9, like I did, and reached the end of their lives without truly having a changed heart. They never actually gave their lives to Christ. I could have died and gone to hell in this state. I thought that I had to be good to go to heaven. This is the fruit of salvation, but not the root. Being good without Christ is not true salvation. The Scripture says, "That if thou shalt confess with thy mouth the Lord Jesus, and shalt believe in thine heart that God hath raised him from the dead, thou shalt be saved. For with the heart man believeth unto righteousness; and with the mouth confession is made unto salvation. For the scripture saith, Whosoever believeth on him shall not be ashamed." (Rom. 10:9-11),

I had to accept Jesus Christ as my personal Lord and Savior and have a renewed heart and mind in order to go to heaven. I had to cut a covenant with God the Father. I believed if the Father began a good work in me, he would complete it.

That work began when I accepted Christ into my life. Salvation is conforming into the image of God's Son. And if the Father starts a work, he will complete it; he is not going to stop until I look just like Christ Jesus.

During the four years I was in college, I gave my life to Christ at least fifty times. I did not know any better. I had a Word deficiency. My idea of salvation was trying to be a good person to please the Lord God. Here I was in college, yet still in kindergarten church school. I was academically smart, but below the bar spiritually.

Since I attended a Baptist institution, there were many seminary students there working on their ministerial degrees. Unknowingly, I chose the same dorm as the seminary students. I did not want to live with all of the athletes, even though I was an athlete myself. They were too noisy and stayed up during all hours of the night. I needed to be in a residence hall that was quiet so I could study.

I enjoyed living with the seminary students. My roommate was really a great guy. He was a Christian. He and I played on the football team together. He drove a motorcycle, played the guitar, sang well, and best of all, he knew how to cook. I was not going to starve to death! My roommate introduced me to a sandwich that literally helped me make it through many hungry nights. The Lord knew what he was doing when he connected me with my roomy. I've often thanked God for his grace, mercy, and protection during my college years.

I know you want to know more about the sandwich. I was momentarily fearful that if included in this book, the recipe would get into the hands of unscrupulous people who might attempt to sell it on the black market. But since I own the copyright to this book, and no part of it may be reproduced without written consent from me, I decided it was safe to share the recipe. Prepare yourself for a little taste of heaven.

The following sandwich is the bread of life, the manna from heaven, the angel's food that my Father provided me during my college years in the wilderness. Do you not know that the sons of God ate angel's food? How do you think they survived?

Banana Sandwich

Ingredients:

2 tbsp. mayonnaise

2 bananas, diced

4-6 slices fresh bread

Combine mayonnaise and diced bananas in a small bowl. Be careful not to make the mixture too creamy. Spread on two or three slices of fresh bread and cover with remaining slices. Turn oven to broil and place two sandwiches on the rack. Watch them closely, as the bread will brown quickly. Once the tops are lightly browned, flip the two sandwiches over until the opposite sides are browned. If you have more sandwiches, repeat the process. Eat while warm--manna from heaven!

Now that I've taught you about physical food, let's continue to graduating from church school. I must have looked like I needed to be saved because every time I turned around, it seemed that another seminary student was trying to lead me to Christ. It got to the point where I asked the Lord, "Why are all of these guys trying to save me?"

I did not have any spiritual sense back then. I did not want to be rude to those I considered children of God, so I accepted their offers of salvation. It would have been rude to tell a seminary student that I had already been saved forty nine times. They were so sincere. And maybe I boosted their confidence by saying yes to the offer of salvation. Who knows? All I realized was that it made them extremely happy.

On the spiritual side, it was hard for me to take some of the seminarians seriously because I saw them smoking, kissing, drinking, cursing, and partying. In other words, these students who were preparing for a life of sharing the good news of God acted no differently from many other college students.

My second year of college, my roommate became a resident assistance and moved out, while one of my football team friends moved in. We roomed together for a year before my best friend from high school transferred to the university and became my roommate. We were having a great time until the day my best friend gave his life to Christ for real. He "got saved" and dramatically changed.

Now I not only had all of the soon-to-be ministers trying to save me, I had my roommate trying to bring me to the Lord as well! What was I to do? The pressure became so immense that I made a deal with the Lord God. You see, the reason I felt I couldn't give my life completely to Christ was because I thought I had to be "clean" first. I also had all these "thou shall not's" from my earlier church years running around in my head. I did not believe I could come to God as I was. I was told that I could, but I did not believe it. So I made a promise to the Lord God that when I graduated from college and got married, I would then give my life to him wholeheartedly, all the while hoping that Jesus would not come back tomorrow.

My college buddies and I formed a Gospel singing group called "The Rising Stars." We traveled to local churches and sang Gospel songs, but it was short lived. Although our group sounded great, none of us were truly saved and this was a problem. My favorite song was "Tomorrow" by the Winans. In the song, it talks about giving your life to Christ tomorrow, but tomorrow might be too late. I prayed frequently for Jesus to not return tomorrow.

One afternoon, after singing at a church, the Holy Spirit reminded me that I could not toy with God. Our singing group was standing at the front of the church, shaking hands with the congregation. As I stood there, an older lady shook hands with the other guys before stopping in front of me. I'll never forget the words she said. "You sounded great. I hope you meant it." My spirit shook, I felt like I was going to fall, and my soul became afraid.

"The fear of the Lord is the beginning of knowledge: but fools despise wisdom and instruction." (Prov. 1:7)

It was at this point that I realize that GOD does not like TWO FACES! You have to choose a side in order to run this race. Which side do you choose?

Afterwards, when our group got in the car and left the church, I told the guys what happened to me and that I was through. I would no longer be singing with the group. They tried to convince me otherwise, telling me that I was making a big deal out of nothing. But none of my friends had experienced the spiritual encounter that I did.

Although the words had come out of the lady's mouth, I knew it was a direct warning from the Lord. I heard the voice of God clearly, with fear and trembling. This was a good thing. The fear, or reverence, of the Lord is not a bad fear. It is a fear and respect for the one that is highly exalted over heaven and earth; fear and respect for the one that has life and death in his hands. His name is Jesus Christ. Do you respect the Lord Jesus Christ?

For the first time in my entire life, I heard what the Spirit of the Lord was saying to me. I feared the Lord God and started cleaning up my life and temple. I did not want the Lord to visit me while I was not ready to open the door of my heart to Him.

As I'm writing this, I've realized the following truth: when the Lord comes to you and he has to knock, this means that your body/temple/house does not belong to him. If it was the Lord's house, he would not have to knock. He would just open the door and walk in. Keep this in mind as you draw closer to him. Does he have to knock or have you made your "house" accessible to him?

In the book of Revelation, Christ Jesus says, "Behold, I stand at the door, and knock: if any man hear my voice, and open the door, I will come in to him, and will sup with him, and he with me. To him that overcometh will I grant to sit with me in my throne, even as I also overcame, and am set down with my Father in his throne. He that hath an ear, let him hear what the Spirit saith unto the churches."

(Rev. 3:20-22)

After sixteen years of school as a student-athlete, I graduated from college in December of 1988. Intellectually, emotionally, and physically, I was fine, but spiritually, I was in kindergarten. After college, I accepted a job in Charlotte, North Carolina, but with no money, no car, and no place to live, I finally had to call the manager and turn down the job.

I felt as though I was going backwards: I had to move back home to Waterloo, South Carolina with my parents. I was also attending my childhood church that I should have graduated from a long time ago. The question that kept running through my head was why did I lack the inspiration to give my life to Christ? It wasn't a lack of religious influences. Up to that point, I had attended different churches and encountered Baptists, Presbyterians, Lutherans, Catholics, AME members, AME Zion members, Holiness members, Jehovah witnesses, Muslims, Pentecostals, and a multitude of seminary students at my Christian college, yet none of these people inspired a change in me.

I answered this question myself. I did not have a good example of a Christian person who truly lived a godly life in Christ. Most of the so-called Christians I encountered had a form of godliness, yet something was always lacking. The only time I saw the pastor was on Sunday or at church functions. I never encountered him during the week, so I didn't know whether he was a good Christian example.

When the Lord God makes me a minister, I remember thinking to myself, I am going to be different. I will make a difference in people's lives, starting with my family. I will be an earthly example for Christ. I want people to see Christ in my words and actions. I want them to see that I honor God in my daily walk and to realize that Jesus Christ is alive and well.

"For the kingdom of God is not in word, but in power." (1 Cor. 4:20)

I believe that when you demonstrate a godly life in Christ, you can influence people to do the same, but you have to be consistent. In Christ, consistent living in godliness is required.

"This is a faithful saying, and these things I will that thou affirm constantly, that they which have believed in God might be careful to maintain good works. These things are good and profitable unto men." (Tit. 3:8)

The more people I demonstrated Christ Jesus to, the more people I influenced. So I started to exercise godliness. The Word became my food and faith was my nourishment. These are the duties of a good minister.

"For bodily exercise profiteth little: but godliness is profitable unto all things, having promise of the life that now is, and of that which is to come." (1 Tim. 4:8)

We are the children of God and God is love. We are the children of love.

"Owe no man any thing, but to love one another: for he that

loveth another hath fulfilled the law." (Rom. 13:8)

We should not owe people love, we should instead give it freely. How can someone call himself a Christian and not show the love of God to others? Love does not hold grudges; love does not hold un-forgiveness. Love does not hate. God loves his children. He says, "As many as I love, I rebuke and chasten: be zealous therefore, and repent." (Rev. 3:19)

God our Father only chastises his children because he loves them. As a father, I do the same: I chastise my children because I love them. I do not chastise another father's children like I would my own. If God does not chastise you, you might not be his child.

Once I was back at home with my parents, I had to come up with a plan to change my situation so that I could move to Charlotte. One night, while my brother Donnie and I were up late watching the movie "Predator" for the eighty-second time, I told him about my plan to leave.

"I'm going to move to Charlotte."

"You can't leave me here, man," he said.

"You better start saving your money then," I replied.

In the words of God, Jesus said, "…If ye have faith, and doubt not…it shall be done." (Matt. 21:21)

In January of 1989, a few weeks after I had graduated from college, I got a job at a local finance company working in management training. Part of my job was repossessing cars from people who were not paying. Repossessing cars was not a fun job, but I was paid to do it. When I received a paycheck, I tried to save every dollar I could. It was going to take a few thousand dollars for me to relocate to Charlotte.

After five months with the finance company, I had almost enough money saved. My dream of moving was about to become a reality. A few months later, I repossessed a nice Carolina blue, Mazda B2000 pickup truck. I bought it ten days later and it became my first vehicle.

As I write this, I am overwhelmed by a flood of memories. I want to thank the Holy Spirit for bringing them up. Although I was still far from the promised land--meaning I had a worldly mindset--I had no debt. Everything that I had purchased up to this point in my life I had paid for in cash. So even though I had the money to pay for my truck, I was advised to purchase it on credit. The financial folks at my company insisted that I needed to begin establishing a credit history. They wanted me to do things the world's way and I listened. This is an essential part of my story, because for me, it became my "way of the cross."

So instead of buying the truck outright, I was set up on a payment plan that I might start building credit history. My truck payments were $152 a month. I was also told that I needed to establish about four or five credit accounts with good paying histories so that my credit report looked good. This way, I could make larger purchases in the future, like buying an expensive car or a house.

Well, I fell for it and the Lord God allowed it. I will tell you why he allowed it a little later on. While attending church school, I had not been taught God's way of doing things financially. I had no knowledge of kingdom finances. So I fell for the world's way of doing things via the credit system.

Now that I had accomplished two of the three things I needed in order to relocate to Charlotte I started to feel good about my move: I had money saved and I had a vehicle. All I needed now was a place to live. I called up a college buddy that was living in Charlotte and he agreed to let me stay with him until I got an apartment.

At the beginning of August, eight months after moving in with my parents, my manager at the finance company informed me that I had accumulated two vacation days. I took this as a golden opportunity to go to Charlotte to look for a job.

My plans were to go up on the weekend and stay with my friend before returning home Tuesday. I went up on Saturday, purchased a newspaper, and got busy circling jobs. I spent all day Monday and Tuesday applying for work and was back at my job on Wednesday. I asked the Lord to show me favor. After spending those four days in Charlotte, I believed in my heart that I would be relocating to North Carolina soon. I had no doubt about it!

At the end of August, I put in my two weeks notice with the finance company and in September of 1989, I was living in Charlotte. In the words of God, Jesus said, "…If ye have faith, and doubt not…it shall be done." (Matt. 21:21)

Two weeks after I moved to Charlotte, Hurricane Hugo hit like a 600-mile wide tornado. I never knew what hit us. Until Hugo's arrival, I did not think that a hurricane could reach this far inland. It devastated North Carolina. I had to live without power for several days, but I survived the storm. I still thought I was in the right place.

The difference between an eagle and a chicken or a doe-doe bird is that the chicken and doe-doe bird run from the storm, while the eagle flies directly into it, catches the storm winds underneath its wings, and rises above. I am like an eagle.

After I established residency in Charlotte, I searched for another church to attend. My friend invited me to his church and I liked it. The church membership was much larger than what I was used to, but the people were friendly.

Two years later, in 1990, I married my high school sweetheart. Shortly after that, I kept my promise to the Lord God and gave my life to Christ. I have to admit that I tried to put the Lord God off at first, pretending I had forgotten my promise to him. But the Holy Spirit kept bringing the promise back to my mind.

"The fear of the Lord is the beginning of knowledge: but fools despise wisdom and instruction." (Prov. 1:7)

I remember exactly how it happened. I was sitting in my car, thinking about the Lord's goodness and how patient he had been with me. I asked him for his forgiveness, repented of all my sins and unrighteousness, and he forgave me, just like that! And most of all, he was not mad at me. Thank you, Lord, for your love.

"That if thou shalt confess with thy mouth the Lord Jesus, and shalt believe in thine heart that God hath raised him from the dead, thou shalt be saved." (Rom. 10:9)

I felt like a brand new man. I began smiling big, just as Mrs. Celie did on The Color Purple when Sug Avery asked her to show her teeth. I sat there in my car, looking in the rearview mirror, showing the Lord God my big, toothy smile and laughing to myself. I could not wait to let somebody know. I told my wife what had happened and she was glad and so proud. That was good enough for me: I was saved.

Because of how I was brought up as a child, I thought my salvation was not truly official until I went before the congregation and repented. So I did. But I was not led to go before the congregation in Charlotte. I was being drawn to go back to the very first church that I had graduated from: my hometown church. I hoped that the Lord God would use me as an example, influencing some of my relatives and friends to give their lives to Christ. The Lord God is good. Afterwards, my wife and I started attending our church in Charlotte on a regular basis.

Lord, I thank you for your patience and grace with me on this road to salvation.

GRADUATING FROM CHURCH SCHOOL

Part 2

6

My sins were forgiven for his name's sake and I was born again on October 16, 1990. I had always known about Jesus, but had never fully accepted him and his saving grace until that day in October. In previous times, I had accepted him with my mouth, but not with my heart and mind. This time was different. I was a new creation and gave myself to him freely. What a feeling! Being a newbie in Christ, I was excited and wanted to share the salvation message with everyone. I desired everyone's salvation.

I felt as if I had finally grown up. I was attending church school, salvation in hand. I could finally sit through a service without feeling anxious about whether or not I was saved. I had, on my own, made the decision to go down to the front of the church and give my life to Christ. I had graduated from a sinner to a Christian. Hallelujah!

As an unsaved person, it used to be hard watching others go to the altar and give their lives to Christ. I felt uncomfortable because I knew I was unsaved. I was living in the hope that Jesus would not return anytime soon. I feared going to hell, but my hope that Christ would wait for me to come to him was stronger than my fear.

I received a revelation that hope is the only thing stronger than fear. There are a lot of people in bondage to hope and I could not live my life that way any longer. I had to graduate from hope to faith.

"Now faith is the substance of things hoped for, the evidence of things not seen." (Heb. 11:1)

The word "substance" is important. "Sub" means underneath, for example submerged or submarine; "stance" means to stand. Substance means under-standing what is unseen or invisible. So faith means understanding that God is God. He is a spirit and I must worship him in spirit and in truth.

As a new Christian, I was excited about life. I had a new life in Charlotte that included a wife, an apartment, a job, and in December of 1990, I was approved for my first credit card. I paid off my truck in seven months because I could not stand having to write a check each month just to establish credit.

But because of the finance company's advice, I thought this is what I had to do to establish credit in order to purchase a house. When I activated my first credit card, it was downhill financially from there. The only way out was the "way of the cross."

Figurately, it took me ten years to travel out of Egypt, downhill alongside the Red Sea, and to a point where I could cross over into the desert. I spent ten long years in the labyrinth of the world's system before I made my way out of the credit system of debt.

Here I was, an intellectual, a college graduate, and a married adult. I was attending church regularly, but my spiritual life was no farther along than the first grade. But I was right where the Lord wanted me to be. I was a blank sheet of paper, a babe in Christ. If I was going to be helped, it was going to take a revelation for babes.

"At that time Jesus answered and said, I thank thee, O Father, Lord of heaven and earth, because thou hast hid these things from the wise and prudent, and hast revealed them unto babes." (Matt. 11:25)

Although I was spiritually in the first grade, I had a gift called comprehension. I had the ability to read God's Word and understand what the Spirit was saying to me.

At first, I was too lazy to meditate on the verses I was reading in my King James Bible. So I purchased a Living Bible, written in a format that was easier to read. I was hungry for the Word of God. I read and read and read that Bible. The stories were so fascinating. It made me wondered why my previous pastors did not preach on the stories I was reading. That really puzzled me.

Then one evening, when I was attending a Bible study, the teacher shared that she was praying for our pastor to read more of the Scriptures from the pulpit. I was floored. I wondered if other people were as puzzled as I was. I began praying for my pastor as well, asking the Lord to encourage him to read more Scriptures. He never did.

After two years of marriage, my wife and I had our first daughter. Fourteen months later, we had our second daughter.

"The Lord bless thee, and keep thee: The Lord make his face shine upon thee, and be gracious unto thee: The Lord lift up his countenance upon thee, and give thee peace. And they shall put my name upon the children of Israel; and I will bless them." (Num. 6:24-27)

For each of these blessings, I praised the Lord. I thanked my Abba Father God for blessing and keeping me; I thanked Jesus for lifting me up and giving me peace; I thanked the Holy Spirit for shining on me and being gracious. In twenty-four months, I went from being single and unsaved, to being saved, married, and a new father. I was going to require the heavenly Hosts' help, as I was now living with girls. I grew up in the country, the oldest of four boys. I had eight uncles and many male cousins; there were very few girls in my family. The girls that were around had to be tough. Initially, I was not very good at dealing with the emotional ups and downs and the sensitivity that girls have in abundance.

For example, one day my daughter was crying for no reason. After I picked her up, she stopped. I did not fall for that emotional trap again. From then on, whenever my daughter cried for me to hold her, I did not pick her up. I would just let her cry herself to sleep. I figured that it was a girl thing and I could outlast a baby crying. Their mother, on the other hand, could not.

I felt I passed a major test in Christ and graduated to the next level. As a father, I cannot be always flustered by my children's feelings. One minute they are happy, the next minute they are sad. They are friends with me, and then I turn around and they are not. Children are unstable in their ways. While this is typical of all children, as a parent, I recognized that my love for them would be unchanging, yet their love for me would change based upon how they felt in the moment.

God our Father acts the same way towards us. He is not shaken by our emotional instability. One minute we are happy, the next we are sad. One minute we are praising him, and the next, we are complaining. We are similar to children. The Holy Spirit is also not influenced by our flighty feelings; his love for us is constant. We read in the Scriptures, however, that Jesus was moved to pity. (Joel 2:10) In the same way that my wife pleads my child's case to me, Jesus pleads your case to the Father.

Using that lesson, I learned how to be a father. I applied the sort of relationships I have with God, Jesus, and the Holy Spirit to the relationship I have with my family. I realized that my family should emulate the image and order of the kingdom of God. God is orderly; we can see that in his creation. He is a God of order. As a child of Christ, I go to Jesus and Jesus, in turn, goes to the Father on my behalf. My children go to their mother and their mother comes to me on their behalf. I know those of you with families can relate to this.

For example, I was driving my family somewhere. My wife was in the passenger seat and my two daughters were in the back. The girls needed to stop and use the restroom. They said, "Mom, we need to go to the bathroom." So my wife said, "Franklin, please stop at the next exit so that the girls can use the bathroom."

The older the girls got, the bolder they became. They started to ask me for things on their own. Although they usually still ask their mother for things first, at times they, "come boldly unto the throne of grace." (Heb. 4:16) This is similar to maturing in Christ. Sooner or later you are required to grow up to the point where you can come boldly to the throne of God and ask the Father for things yourself.

How does it look for a full-grown man to be afraid to go directly to his dad and talk to him? It is fine to talk to Jesus, and the Holy Spirit is with us always, but sometimes I want to talk directly to my Father God. In this way, I am thankful that I no longer have fear! I thank you, Holy Spirit, for allowing me to graduate from church school. The more I studied and meditated on the Word of God, the more I realized that my life was still not in proper alignment with the Spirit of God.

Although I was saved, I still controlled my life. I was not consistently following the Holy Spirit; I was still catering to my own whims. When I first received salvation, I was doing well, much better than I had in the past. But once I saw how other Christians were acting, I changed my mind. For example, I felt Christians should not be drinking and going to clubs in the evenings. However, my fellow brothers in Christ were doing this, so I began to think it must be okay to be saved and still do these things. Of course, I always added the caveat, "it's okay as long as I do not overdo it."

I was still walking in sense knowledge instead of revelation knowledge, meaning that things had to make sense to me before I could truly believe them. I was depending on my senses in order to believe, but faith doesn't make sense. Walking on water does not make sense, yet it creates faith. The burning bush does not make sense, but it creates faith.

I did not understand about becoming dead to sin. I was called to recognize that my old life was dead, this much I knew. It was only by the grace of God that I knew my old life was gone. So I prayed to the Holy Spirit to help me really comprehend what God required of me.

The Lord spoke to me and said that I was reading Scripture too fast. He urged me to slow down. I purposely began to read slowly. Once I paced myself and began meditating, analyzing, and studying the Word, it was as if the Lord God had unplugged my ears and taken the scales off of my eyes. I began to understand.

Have you ever had the experience of someone explaining something in a new way and you respond, "Oh, now I see!" That's how your faith should be.

Satan doesn't want us to receive revelations from God. But God does. The Word of God says, "For he that is dead is freed from sin. Now if we be dead with Christ, we believe that we shall also live with him: Knowing that Christ being raised from the dead die no more; death hath no more dominion over him. For in that he died, he died unto sin once: but in that he live, he live unto God. Likewise reckon you also yourselves to be dead indeed unto sin, but alive unto God through Jesus Christ our Lord." (Rom. 6:7-11)

"For the wages of sin is death; but the gift of God is eternal life through Jesus Christ our Lord." (Rom. 6:23)

"There is therefore now no condemnation to them which are in Christ Jesus, who walk not after the flesh, but after the Spirit. For the law of the Spirit of life in Christ Jesus hath made me free from the law of sin and death." (Rom. 8:1)

I am not afraid of death. Death is afraid of me because I am raised from the dead in Christ. As a Christian, I have eternal life in Christ, whereas death has an end. Death is not eternal. Satan and his host will be consumed in the lake of fire.

The more I meditated on what I was reading, the more I learned. I studied the Bible thoroughly. I divided difficult words and looked up the definitions using my concordance, I studied maps, and I read supplemental materials. I realized that my biggest obstacle was my mindset. So I started learning about the differences between the carnal mindset verses the spiritual mindset. I wanted to be spiritually minded so that I could know the truth. More importantly, I wanted to please the Lord God by living a godly life so that I could be in heaven with him one day.

I had to graduate from my carnal mindset to a spiritual mindset so that I could mature into the sonship of believers.

"For as many as are led by the Spirit of God, they are the sons of God. For ye have not received the spirit of bondage again to fear; but ye have received the Spirit of adoption, whereby we cry, Abba, Father. The Spirit itself beareth witness with our spirit, that we are the children of God...." (Rom. 8:14-16)

As an adopted son of the Father, I knew what the Lord wanted from me: he wanted everything. He wanted me to put aside the things of this world.

"For they that are after the flesh do mind the things of the flesh; but they that are after the Spirit the things of the Spirit. For to be carnally minded is death; but to be spiritually minded is life and peace. Because the carnal mind is enmity against God: for it is not subject to the law of God, neither indeed can be. So then they that are in the flesh cannot please God." (Rom. 8:5-8)

When I meditated on these Scriptures, I knew I was going to need spiritual persuasion. I wanted to be fully persuaded that neither death, nor life, nor angels, nor principalities, nor powers, nor things present, nor things to come, nor height, nor depth, nor any other creature would be able to separate me from the love of God, which is in Christ Jesus our Lord (Rom. 8:38-39).

But becoming spiritually minded does not come easy. The best things in life never are until you get into God's class. Then everything becomes incredibly easy because you are not doing the work; the Word of God, with the Holy Spirit's help, enlightens your mind. And the most difficult thing is to believe without doubt. I challenge you to come in! The door to the kingdom of God is open to those who are willing to cast aside doubt and believe in Christ Jesus.

I had to get into shape. There was no way I would succeed in beating down the enemy in my current spiritual shape. I needed a godly spiritual trainer. I had attended church school all of my life and I had never heard a pastor preach on godliness. As I thought about whom I could go to for training, my mind drew a blank. Then the Holy Spirit reminded me that the Word purifies.

"Now the Spirit speaketh expressly, that in the latter times some shall depart from the faith, giving heed to seducing spirits, and doctrines of devils; Speaking lies in hypocrisy [false teachers]; having their conscience seared with a hot iron [insensibility]...." (1 Tim. 4:1-2)

There was only one trainer who could prepare me and his name was the Holy Spirit.

"For bodily exercise profiteth little: but godliness is profitable unto all things, having promise of the life that now is, and of that which is to come. This is a faithful saying and worthy of all acceptation." (1 Tim. 4:8-9)

Spiritual exercise began by stretching my prayer life. Stretching included Bible study, meditation, fasting, trusting, and believing. So I continued with this course of study until the Spirit of the Lord urged me to work towards a higher level in Christ. I knew I was going to encounter challenges. It requires hardship for a believer to delve deeper into the mysteries of faith. In Christ, your loss is your gain. You have to lose the world's way of doing things to gain the kingdom of God. This is a truth experienced by many who believe. If I was going to be a soldier in God's army, I couldn't place limits on myself or on the Lord. I couldn't experience God's power by being timid.

It was at this point in my spiritual walk that I knew there was going to be adversity. Whenever the Lord God leads you to a place where you need to cross over, you should be aware of the dangers lurking about. This danger can disguise itself in many different ways, such as in pharaoh's army in the past, the Federal army today, or for some, in the form of creditors. Or the dangers waiting in the murky waters of life can be the devil's army, vices, addictions, or other false beliefs. The way to the promised land is littered with adversities like these. This is the "way of the cross." Jesus is the way, the truth, and the life. It is through his courts of praise and through our difficulties that we become one with him. This is more powerful than we can imagine. It is through the tabernacle; it is through his blood; it is through Christ Jesus. There is only one way to the Father and it is through his son, Jesus the Christ.

Have you ever wondered how pharaoh's army (the federal government and the world credit system) and the enemy's army all know the exact spot where you will be crossing over the river? Pharaoh will let you go. In fact, he will lure you with great promises, and then send the army of creditors to prevent you from crossing over the Red Sea to the promised land. Fear not! The Lord God is with you and he wants you to cross over safely and be debt free. For the believer, the Lord God will open up the sea and allow you to walk across on dry land.

In the animal kingdom, the wild beasts have to cross over the river in order to survive famine and get to greener pastures. The caribous have to cross over the frozen tundra. The enemy knows the spots well. The alligators and crocodiles get to the river weeks earlier and wait on the smaller beasts to cross. The wolves trail the caribous across the tundra. All animals' lives are at stake, so every year, around the same time, they run to the same place to cross over.

For me, there is only one way to make it, and this is what is known as the "way of the cross." Each person must decide whether he is willing to take the risk to cross over. Are you willing to forsake all, even knowing the enemy is closing in behind you or waiting in the waters to devour you?

Looking at my behavior and those of my fellow Christians, it was horrible that we found it all right to be ministers, deacons, choir members, ushers, or leaders in the church and still drink, smoke, curse, party, fornicate, and backbite. We were no different than nonbelievers and I readily fell into this trap with the others. I should have graduated from this church as soon as I became a believer, yet sadly, I stayed. I was involved in several ministries and I did not know how to break the news to the pastor and my friends that we were leaving. That was the last time I would be disobedient to the Holy Spirit. He kept telling me to leave that church where he did not truly reign in the hearts of his people.

An entire year went by and I went through a trial for my disobedience. It tested my faith. It was as if the Holy Spirit abandoned me, waiting to see what I would do.

I woke up one day, thoroughly fed up with how I was living. I was doing whatever I wanted to do, yet feeling frustrated and dissatisfied. I was working hard and making decent money, but I was unable to see the fruit of my labor because I had credit card debt. The majority of my money was going toward paying creditors, utilities, taxes, and insurance. It had gotten to the point where I could not see my way out and I was sick and tired of being sick and tired. I felt as though I was in captivity to the credit system and it was affecting both me and my family.

So I prayed. I cried out to the Lord God and sought him with all my heart. He heard my cry and said, "Franklin, I have been thinking about you." I took this personally.

"Lord, you have been thinking about me?" I answered.

"I know the thoughts that I have toward you, Franklin," the Lord responded.

"For I know the thoughts that I think toward you, saith the Lord, thoughts of peace, and not of evil, to give you an expected end. Then shall ye call upon me, and ye shall go and pray unto me, and I will hearken unto you. And ye shall seek me, and find me, when ye shall search for me with all your heart. And I will be found of you, saith the Lord: and I will turn away your captivity, and I will gather you from all the nations, and from all the places whither I have driven you, saith the Lord; and I will bring you again into the place whence I cause you to be carried away captive." (Jer. 29:11-14)

It was during this spiritual encounter that the Holy Spirit baptized me with fire. He revealed to me that it was the Lord God who led me into captivity. God allowed me to get pulled into the credit system that I might be trained. He knew I'd be frustrated and eventually come to the realization that he is the only source I should depend on, not the world's system. I was taught that I cannot serve both God and mammon (money). So I chose to serve the Lord God.

Attending church from this point on was significantly different. I could not pay attention to the stories the pastor was sharing because they were irrelevant to me. The pastor was not teaching me anything. During his preaching, I would be reading my Bible. I was being inspired by the Holy Spirit and writing notes on what he was teaching me.

I knew that the Holy Spirit didn't want me to waste my time by attending that church anymore. During this time, I felt the Lord God calling me to carry out his administrative work, but first, I had to align my life according to the qualifications of deacons, as stated in the book of Timothy. As I was lining up my life, the pastor invited me to become a deacon. This was a direct confirmation of the Lord's private revelation to me! To be invited to be a deacon is an honor and with this, comes great expectation to serve the Lord faithfully.

So I said yes and studied for the next year to be a deacon.

As I went through the training, I tried to discern if there were others there that I could recognize as deacons of Christ. In the group of fifty candidates, I could not find one that was a deacon for Christ. There were plenty who met the qualifications to become a deacon at this particular church. As a matter of fact, another lady and I were the only two people who had perfect class attendance. Yes, I said "lady."

After I had completed the course, my spirit would not allow me to be ordained at this church. When I informed the pastor that I would not be at the ordination service, and that my family and I were moving on, he was upset. He had noticed my maturity in Christ. He said that there was something different about me. He had noticed a godly character that he and others loved. I was flattered, but I didn't tell the pastor that the Lord had already ordained me as a deacon for the Body of Christ, and not just for the local church.

Although I loved the people at my church and enjoyed my involvement in the various ministries, the Lord had other plans for me. I had to follow God's leadings. I had spent much of my life doing what I wanted to do and now it was time to follow God, no matter how painful. The more I studied the Word of God, the more frustrated I became with traditional church. It was time to graduate. As I participated in the conclusion of the final service I was to attend at that church, I said to myself, "It is finished." And just like that, I graduated from my second church. Thank you, Holy Spirit!

Because the Holy Spirit had been my instructor, I had spiritually matured beyond preaching. Even when the pastor tried to convince me to stay, my mind was already made up. Puzzled, he asked me to explain my change of heart. I privately shared what the Lord had been doing in my life. I told him that the Lord had helped me mature to a higher level of spirituality and that he was calling me to a deeper walk. My pastor was offended. He said, "Do you think that I am not spiritual? You are just on a high right now, but it will cool down!"

Oh, I needed to hear that! It was just the confirmation I needed to know that I had made the right decision to leave. Thank you, Pastor, for the fuel!

7

The Lord God visited me in a dream one night and gave me another chance to change my ways and follow him. In my dream, I was fishing with my friend Cedric, my dad, and my dad's friend, Bird. There was this giant fish with huge teeth that tried to bite me when I pulled it out of the water. A giant bear was sleeping underneath a log pile and when the bear heard the commotion with the fish, he woke up. Once the bear saw us, he charged after Cedric and me. He did not chase after my dad and Bird.

As Cedric and I ran through the woods, we came to a large log fence that was about forty feet tall. We had to climb a ladder to get to the other side. I got to the ladder first and scaled up quickly. When I crossed the fence to the other side, I heard Cedric yell, letting me know that he was stuck, straddling the top of the fence. I quickly climbed back up to free him, just before the giant bear could grab him.

Once we were on the ground, we ran to the SUV. My dad and Bird opened the doors and Cedric dove in first, but as I approached the car, a tiger appeared out of nowhere and blocked the door. I ran around to the other side of the car, but he moved quickly and blocked my way. Suddenly, I saw an opening. I dove inside the car. As we drove off, I said loudly, "I WISH A TIGER WOODS!"

The interpretation is this: you cannot straddle the fence with God or be of two faces. You have to make a choice. Which side you are going to be on? My friend and I were straddling the fence between righteousness and unrighteousness. The Holy Spirit came to convict us of righteousness in Christ. Glory be to God that we chose righteousness. It was at this point that I felt the Lord God giving me my robe of righteousness. Thank you, Abba Father.

Being baptized with water is symbolic of being baptized with fire. Every believer in Christ has to go through the fire and be baptized with the Holy Spirit. It is a part of the process of graduating from church school. There is a difference between being baptized with natural water by a pastor and being baptized with the Holy Spirit and with fire by Christ Jesus. The pastor cannot baptize you with the Holy Spirit and with fire like Jesus can, but he can pray to the Lord to bless you. You can pray yourself for an infilling of God's Spirit.

John the Baptist said, "I indeed baptize you with water unto repentance: but he that cometh after me is mightier than I, whose shoes I am not worthy to bear: he shall baptize you with the Holy Ghost, and with fire: Whose fan is in his hand, and he will thoroughly purge his floor, and gather his wheat into the garner; but he will burn up the chaff with unquenchable fire." (Matt. 3:11-12)

The eternal fire is the future of the wicked. Do you want to be baptized by the man from Galilee? His name is Jesus. Jesus traveled from Galilee to the Jordan. In this way, he was baptized by John, fulfilling the Scriptures. I see the Scripture passage above as an example of graduating from church school and then trusting the Holy Spirit and following him.

John the Baptist's job was to point you to Christ. Once he steered you in that direction, his job was done: he expected you to start following Jesus. Humbly, Jesus went to be anointed. This was the beginning of his public ministry. While the anointing came about through John's prayers, the power came from God the Father who, through the Spirit (symbolized by the dove) said, "…This is my beloved Son, in whom I am well pleased; hear ye him." (Matt. 17:5)

You are to follow Christ. There is no one else. Maybe the pastor can point you to Christ, but we are not to follow a specific pastor or elevate him to a position that is above the Lord. Jesus is the good news. Hallelujah to the Lamb of God, the Lion of Judah.

The Jordan River is a place of transition, a place where you cross over. We must cross over from lusting after the carnal things of the flesh to following the things of the Spirit. Jesus' baptism by John, a mere man, symbolizes his death, burial, and resurrection.

The next time you are at a baptism, look for these three things. When the person steps down into the water and stands, ready to be baptized, he is to cross his arms over his chest. This represents death. The baptizer says the following, "I baptize you in the name of the Father, the Son, and the Holy Spirit" and dips the person into the water. This represents burial (laying you down to rest). Finally, the person is raised out of the water. This represents resurrection in Christ.

Being baptized with water means you have to come out of the water. Being baptized with the Holy Spirit and with fire means you stay in Christ and you do not come out. You are raised up in him and now you abide in him and he in you. You are a new creature. Behold, old things are passed away and all things become new.

"There is one body, and one Spirit, even as ye are called in one hope of your calling: One Lord, one faith, one baptism, One God and Father of all, who is above all, and through all, and in you all. But unto every one of us is given grace according to the measure of the gift of Christ." (Eph. 4:4-7)

Most saved people never get to the point where they are baptized by the Holy Spirit and with fire. As a matter of fact, most people consider salvation to consist of repeating Romans 10:9 and being baptized by water. This is only the first part of the process (the first baptism).

As a sinner, you trod a broad path and think that there are many ways to get to heaven. When you give your life to Christ, you are saved by grace. But there is a lot more to the Lord God. As a saved person, your path gets narrower because you start to believe that Jesus is the only way. On this path, you must be baptized again by the Holy Spirit and with fire. As a saved person, you still have the proclivity to succumb to the things of the flesh. Proclivity means "tendency or leaning or bending." In other words, you are two faces. Sometimes, you are in your flesh and sometimes you are in the spirit. Either way, you remain lukewarm and self-satisfied. God will spew the lukewarm out of his mouth, Scripture tells us. You have to be for him or against him; hot or cold. (Rev. 3:15-16)

In order to get on the narrow path and be a true saint of God, you must be tried by the fire of the Holy Spirit. After that occurs, you will find yourself on the narrow path because you now believe that there is only one way to the Father and that is through Jesus Christ. This is narrow-minded thinking, which is why it is called the narrow way.

The Holy Spirit brings fire to purge your sin. As a Christian, I was still lured by the things of the flesh. I was not fit for the kingdom of God. In order to become fit for the kingdom, the Holy Spirit had to come upon me with his holy fire and purify me.

When the Holy Spirit purifies in fire, I'm not removed until I am like gold. This happens when he looks into the fire and sees his reflection in me. Unlike stubble, hay, or wood, which are consumed by fire, gold shines brighter. Gold is redemption.

Every minister should go through a prophetic process in order to be a good leader of the Lord's people. However, many are found lacking. In order to meet God the Father, you must be prepared.

As I matured in Christ, I realized there was a progression: I had transitioned from a child in Christ, to a grown-up son in Christ, and finally, to a father in Christ. As a child in Christ, I walked the Romans road to salvation by attempting to live in Christ. As a son in Christ, I followed the way, the truth, and the life in order to understand the sacrifice Jesus Christ had made. I was amazed by the abundance of grace and the mercy that our Savior had for me. As a father in Christ, I went through the believer's walk of faith, learning how to imitate my daddy, God the Father. I began to walk in the power and the authority that he gave me, becoming consistent and conducting myself in his character.

(Child)

The Romans Road to Salvation

1. Rom. 3:10: "As it is written, There is none righteous, no, not one...."

2. Rom. 3:23: "For all have sinned, and come short of the glory of God...."

3. Rom. 5:8: But God commendeth his love toward us, in that, while we were yet sinners, Christ died for us."

4. Rom. 5:12: "Wherefore, as by one man sin entered into the world, and death by sin; and so death passed upon all men, for that all have sinned."

5. Rom. 5:19: "For as by one man's disobedience many were made sinners, so by the obedience of one shall many be made righteous."

6. Rom. 6:23: "For the wages of sin is death; but the gift of God is eternal life through Jesus Christ our Lord."

7. Rom. 10:9: "That if thou shalt confess with thy mouth the Lord Jesus, and shalt believe in thine heart that God hath raised him from the dead, thou shalt be saved."

8. Rom. 10:17: "So then faith cometh by hearing, and hearing by the word of God."

9. Rom. 12:1: "I beseech you therefore, brethren, by the mercies of God, that ye present your bodies a living sacrifice, holy, acceptable unto God, which is your reasonable service."

10. Rom. 12:2: "And be not conformed to this world: but be ye transformed by the renewing of your mind, that ye may prove what is that good, and acceptable, and perfect, will of God."

11. Rev. 3:20: "Behold, I stand at the door, and knock: if any man hear my voice, and open the door, I will come in to him, and will sup with him, and he with me."

(Son)

The Way, The Truth, and The Life

"Enter into his gates with thanksgiving, and into his courts with praise: be thankful unto him, and bless his name. For the Lord is good; his mercy is everlasting; and his truth endureth to all generations." (Ps. 100:4-5)

Welcome to the outer court…

The brazen altar through the fire…

The Lover washing with the Word…

Most people are out here in the natural light and never get to go into the Inner court.

Welcome to the Inner court…

The Candlestick…

The Table of Showbread…

The Altar of Incense…

Welcome to the Holy of Holies…

The Mercy Seat…

The Cherubims…

The Mercy Seat is overlaid with Gold. The Gold covers the wood…

Jesus' Blood is on the Mercy Seat. God only sees the Blood. The only thing that God cannot see through is the Blood of Jesus. The Blood covers our sin.

(Father)

The Characteristics of the Believer's Walk of Faith

1. New Life--Rom. 6:4: "Therefore we are buried with him by baptism into death: that like as Christ was raised up from the dead by the glory of the Father, even so we also should walk in newness of life."

2. Faith--2. Cor. 5:7: "(For we walk by faith, not by sight:)"

3. Spirituality--Gal. 5:16: "This I say then, Walk in the Spirit, and ye shall not fulfill the lust of the flesh."

4. Consistency--Eph. 4:1: "I therefore, the prisoner of the Lord, beseech you that ye walk worthy of the vocation wherewith ye are called…."

5. Love--Eph. 5:2: "And walk in love, as Christ also hath loved us, and hath given himself for us an offering and a sacrifice to God for a sweetsmelling savour."

6. Caution--Eph. 5:15: "See then that ye walk circumspectly, not as fools, but as wise…."

7. Illumination--1 John. 1:7: "But if we walk in the light, as he is in the light, we have fellowship one with another, and the blood of

Jesus Christ his Son cleanseth us from all sin."

8. Christ's likeness--1 John. 2:6: "He that saith he abideth in him ought himself also so to walk, even as he walked."

>Folks want to mess with me,
>But they don't know my destiny.
>Son of Man,
>In His hand,
>That's where the blessing will be.
>Let me see,
>Can you trust Him totally?
>He's sure to see,
>You,
>Me.
>In the five-fold ministry,
>It's destiny.
>He's blessing me.
>Forty days and forty nights,
>He's testing me.
>Subjecting me,
>Water, no bread.
>Only the Word was I fed,

The devil was in my head.

He was talking so much,

All I could hear was what he said.

I'm in pain,

But God will sustain.

Maintain.

I'm no longer blind,

Through this, I have survived.

Song of Franklin (SOF)

8

The book of Revelation is one that many Christians have trouble with because it is, in essence, a litmus test. This particular book is Christ's message to the church. Je`sus Christos! Christ reigns! Prayerfully read Revelation and ask the Holy Spirit to enlighten your mind.

Before you continue, read the first three chapters of Revelation. Below, I have provided a breakdown of the key points in those three chapters.

One – Church of Ephesus

The active church was sound in doctrine, but deficient in love.

The Lord approved of the way the church could not bear evil and of how she uncovered the false apostles and liars. He also approved of the hatred for the deeds of the Nicolaitanes.

"Nic-o" means to lord over; "-la-i-tanes" means the lay people.

"Nicolaitanes" means to lord over the lay people. God despises this practice.

The Test

Nevertheless, the Lord God disapproved of the church of Ephesus because the people abandoned their first love; they backslid into sin. They needed to repent and do the first works, or the Lord God would come quickly and remove their candlestick (the candlestick refers to the light of revelation. You need light to see in the dark places. The light reveals the darkness of the soul.).

"He that hath an ear, let him hear what the Spirit saith unto the churches; To him that overcometh (graduates from church school) will I give to eat of the tree of life, which is in the midst of the paradise of God." (Rev. 2:7)

Two – Church of Smyrna

The poor but rich church

Those who are false will be tested.

The Test

False profession, or blasphemy, is saying you are something that you are not. In the Scriptures, Jews were continuously tried—they were the chosen people, yet they kept failing the tests that God put before them. They were swayed by the temptations of the devil. You need to study this to show yourself approved. You will be tested by the devil.

"Fear none of those things which thou shalt suffer: behold, the devil shall cast some of you into prison, that ye may be tried; and ye shall have tribulation ten days: be thou faithful unto death, and I will give thee a crown of life." (Rev. 2:11)

Three – Church of Pergamos
The heretical church

Beware of evil association amongst you. The Lord God's mouth has life and death in it. His mouth is a sharp sword with two edges. Repent for having this evil association or he will come against you with the sword of his mouth. He that overcomes will be able to eat the hidden manna (spiritual food) and be given a new name (Franklin is my new name).

The Test

Professed believers are contrary to an established view, doctrine, or principle. These people can be stumbling blocks. They associate with evil and hold onto false doctrine and they will be condemned. The professed believers upheld the doctrines of the Nicolaitanes, which the Lord despised. Repentance is necessary or the Lord will use the double edged sword of his Word against you.

Four – Church of Thyatira

The church of the false prophetess

Good works are negated because of the association with evil women. Jezebel called herself a prophetess, but she falsely taught and seduced the Lord's servants to commit fornication and eat food sacrificed to idols. The men of today are doing good works, and yet continue to eat the food of the false gods. These foods are drinking, credit cards, expensive cars, overpriced houses, excessive jewelry, perfume, clothes, etc. The Lord God gave Jezebel space to repent, but she did not.

The Test

Those that committed adultery with the false prophetess were cast into a great tribulation. There was no reprieve unless they repented of their deeds. The Lord also allowed for the killing of her children. The power to overcome temptation is given to those who keep the Lord's work until the end; it is the power over nations. And he shall rule with an iron rod and the Lord will give him the morning star, meaning spiritual light. He that has ears needs to hear what the Spirit says to the churches.

Five – Church of Sardis

The dying church

The Lord knows the works that you have done. These include formalism, false profession, and being dead to sin.

The Test

Be watchful, be strong, and do not perform with half-heartedness. The Lord has not found your works perfect before God. If you overcome, you shall be clothed in white and your name will not be blotted out of the book of life.

Six – Church of Philadelphia
The loyal church

The Lord knows your works. He knows a man's heart and has an open door for you. Keep his Word and do not deny his name. And if you have been patient and kept his Word, you will not have to go through the hour of temptation and trials, which shall come upon the entire world at the end of time. Thank you, loyal one, for sticking with God.

No Test

There is no test. Hallelujah! If you overcome, the Lord will make you a pillar in his temple. He will write his name and city on you, who are the new Jerusalem.

Seven – Church of Laodiceans
The lukewarm, self-satisfied church

The Lord knows your works are neither cold nor hot. He wants you to be cold or hot. For those who are lukewarm, he will spew you out of his mouth. This is because you say you are rich and need nothing. You do not realize how wretched, miserable, poor in spirit, blind, and naked you are. As many as God loves, he also rebukes and chastens. Be zealous and repent. [Private Revelation: A father only chastises his own children. He does not chastise someone else's. If God loves you and chastises you, you are his child. If you are not being chastised by God for doing wrong, you are not his child.]

The Test

"Behold, I stand at the door, and knock: if any man hear my voice, and open the door, I will come in to him, and will sup with him, and he with me. To him that overcometh will I grant to sit with me in my throne, even as I also overcame, and am set down with my Father in his throne. He that hath an ear, let him hear what the Spirit saith unto the churches." (Rev. 3:20-22)

9

As a young son of the Lord and a graduate from church school, this verse particularly impacted me: "…because ye are strong, and the word of God abideth in you, and ye have overcome the wicked one." (1 John 2:14)

I was in a new phase of my walk with the Lord. I did not attend church for a time. Instead, I went through a period of studying, meditating, praying, and fasting on my own. I continued to mature in the Lord.

The Holy Spirit was teaching me how the Word applied to my life. I believed what the Lord God was saying to me spiritually. I thought about what my last pastor had said about being on a "spiritual high" and that eventually, I would "cool down." It didn't make sense to me. How in the world is the Holy Spirit, who purifies with fire, going to cool down? No way! No how!

It was at this point, as I realized his unconditional love for me, that I fell in love with the Lord God in a deeper way. I knew he loved me so much that he gave me his only begotten son and I wanted to show this great love of God to others. I wanted everyone I was in contact with to realize how much God loved them. God is pure love and love covers all sin. It was as if I had become a new Christian all over again, with all the enthusiasm of one who wants to shout from the rooftops about God's love for all of humanity. This was what the private time of study and contemplation did for my faith. It grew outside of any boundaries I had previously placed on it before, and my faith knew no end.

As the Lord God prepared my spirit to carry on his admonition, he also prepared me to be a living example of someone who believed in him. The Holy Spirit purified my spirit to hold the mystery of the faith in as pure of a conscience as possible. I had proved myself to him by listening and doing as he directed. I felt that he had ordained me to be a deacon of Christ–even though I had not gone through a formal church ceremony after my studies.

"For they that have used the office of a deacon well purchase to themselves a good degree, and great boldness in the faith which is in Christ Jesus." (1 Tim. 3:13)

Christ Jesus and godliness are my new standard.

"And without controversy great is the mystery of godliness:

God was manifest in the flesh, justified in the Spirit, seen of angels, preached unto the Gentiles, believed on in the world, received up into glory." (1 Tim. 3:16)

I will forever be thankful to the Lord God for never giving up and for growing me in faith enough to trust me to become a steward of the Gospel.

"According to the glorious gospel of the blessed God, which was committed to my trust. And I thank Christ Jesus our Lord, who hath enabled me, for that he counted me faithful, putting me into the ministry...." (1 Tim. 1:11-12)

The Lord God prepared me to go through this phase to test my love for him. I call this the test of love.

"Now the end of the commandment is charity (love) out of a pure heart, and of a good conscience, and of faith unfeigned: From which some having swerved have turned aside unto vain jangling; Desiring to be teachers of the law; understanding neither what they say, nor whereof they affirm." (1 Tim. 1:5-7)

"This is a faithful saying, and worthy of all acceptation, that Christ Jesus came into the world to save sinners; of whom I am chief." (1 Tim. 1:15)

I finally understood with extreme clarity that Christ Jesus came into this world to save sinners and that the church was falling short of this mission. I realized that the activities I was involved in at church every Sunday were fluff. Many of these activities garnered no results, other than to keep me so busy that I did not have time to really study the Word on my own! I had confused activity with results. Week after week, there were people at church who, while touting their own salvation were busy praying for the salvation of others. I witnessed those who claimed salvation coming up to the altar and crying out to the Lord for financial blessings, healings, and a changed heart for a wayward husband. And here I was, trying to minister to those who should already know what salvation was, but didn't. That is not the way of the kingdom.

"Now unto the King eternal, immortal, invisible, the only wise God, be honour and glory for ever and ever. Amen." (1 Tim. 1:17)

It was fitting that the next church I attended focused more on my spiritual growth. The pastor at my new church made me aware of the nature of my spirit and led me to maturity in this way. I felt this was another confirmation from the Lord. In prayer, he had already prepared me spiritually and he had ordained me to be a deacon for the body of Christ. I had a strong sense this was for more than the local church.

This was an exciting time for me. I was learning from someone who understood the nature of the human spirit. The pastor preached sermons that had spiritual significance and were uplifting. He believed in prayer, praise, worship, and fasting. He challenged me and I happily took on the spiritual challenges. Once, he invited the congregation to an all-night prayer vigil. I accepted. On a separate occasion, he challenged the congregation to an all-night praise and worship session. I accepted. He then challenged the congregation to fast for a period of time. I accepted.

Although I had fasted before, that last challenge was to go without eating anything for three days. I was successful and it changed my life forever. Because of this rigorous activity, I now have domination over my body and it does not control me. During that time, I survived on water alone. I now know that my body can go for three days without food. I did not enjoy the fast, but it stretched my faith. This shows what a good pastor can do—he can stretch us beyond the possible and show us that, when going through the impossible, our eyes must rest entirely on Christ to bring us to new heights.

During this time of fasting and self-denial, the Holy Spirit began to test my ability to hear and understand him. He started speaking to me in a heavenly language. It was the spiritual language that I had been studying. It is an unknown tongue to many, but I could understand what the Spirit was saying; it was as if it was in plain English.

I am not talking about the gift of tongues that you may hear some people speaking in evangelical or charismatic churches or even on Christian television programming. I am talking about having an ear to hear what the Spirit of the Lord was saying to me without having to break it down by using worldly examples. He started to speak to me through the Word of God, usually during my meditations. The Lord would ask questions and I would answer him spiritually (within my mind). Then I would answer him carnally, or in the flesh, by demonstrating that I could tell another person what he had revealed to me.

If I spoke the heavenly language in English to someone, they would not understand what I was saying. I would have to tell them what I was saying by using examples, like Jesus with the parables. The best way I can explain this is to give you an example. It is as if two mortgage professionals were talking about mortgages, and then in walks an insurance agent. He does not have a clue what they are saying, although they are speaking in English. The two mortgage professionals would have to translate to the insurance agent what they were saying.

This is how it would sound to the insurance agent: "Once I complete the 1084 and the wage earner tool, I plan to execute the 4506t result. If there are unreimbursed expenses, I will have to review the transcripts. If the cbr shows an initial alert, I will not be able to complete the process until I verify the alert. Once the initial alert is cleared, please escalate to a 4C to sign off on the 4506t results."

While you may understand specific words, unless you have training in the mortgage business, it sounds like a foreign language. The mortgage professional has an ear to hear. In a similar way, we must be vigilant, listen to the Lord, and hear what the Spirit says unto the churches. We must give the Lord time to help us grow in wisdom as we study and pray.

As I continued to pray in the Spirit, I understood more and more about how the kingdom of God works. And with the help of the Holy Spirit, he continued to reveal that the kingdom of God works by asking. If I needed something from the King, the only thing I had to do was to ask him.

"ASK" means A-sk, S-eek, K-nock. You must come to him asking or as-king. Jesus left us his legacy of peace.

"Peace I leave with you, my peace I give unto you: not as the world giveth, give I unto you. Let not your heart be troubled, neither let it be afraid." (John 14:27)

Since I had received peace from the Prince of Peace, all I had to do when I felt anxious was to speak peace to my spirit by reciting this verse: "Let not your heart be troubled...." (John 14:1) And I followed that with, "For God hath not given us the spirit of fear; but of power, and of love, and of a sound mind." (2 Tim. 1:7) These verses I say in the presence of anxiety. Thank you, Holy Spirit, for peace.

There are only three reasons why Jesus came into the world (parenthesis are my own): "...[to] reprove the world of sin, and of righteousness, and of judgment: Of sin, because they (sinners) believe not on me; Of righteousness, because I go to my Father, and ye see me no more; Of judgment, because the prince of this world (Satan) is judged." (John. 16:8-12)

Notice the word "reprove." It means to prove again. What the Spirit of the Lord is saying to us is that these three things, sin, righteousness, and judgment, have already been proven. But since most people do not want to believe this, he is going to reprove it—prove it again, to this age. "He that hath an ear, let him hear what the Spirit saith unto the churches." (Rev. 3:22)

The pastor soon recognized the Spirit of God within me, and asked me to be a deacon and go through the ordination service. I explained that the Lord God had previously blessed me by allowing me to start the process of becoming a deacon, even though he would not allow me to become ordained at the previous church I had attended. I informed him that I would pray to discern what the Lord wanted me to do.

After prayerfully considering the offer, I informed him that I would like to be ordained while at the spiritual retreat at the Billy Graham Training Center in Asheville, North Carolina. My pastor agreed. I did not know what to expect from the Holy Spirit, but I did expect him to meet me there on top of that mountain. So I started fasting and praying in preparation.

"Wherewithal shall a young man cleanse his way? by taking heed thereto according to thy word. With my whole heart have I sought thee: O let me not wander from thy commandments. Thy word have I hid in mine heart, that I might not sin against thee. Blessed art thou, O Lord: teach me thy statutes. With my lips have I declared all the judgments of thy mouth. I have rejoiced in the way of thy testimonies, as much as in all riches. I will meditate in thy precepts, and have respect unto thy ways. I will delight myself in thy statutes: I will not forget thy word." (Ps. 119:9-16)

I was so excited about what the Lord God was about to do in my life that I could hardly contain it. I just continued to thank him every day for what I felt he was about to reveal to me on top of that mountain! When the day finally arrived to drive to the Blue Ridge Mountains, my excitement was slowly replaced by a sense of peace. After my wife and I arrived at the main gate of the retreat center, The Cove, I felt the presence of the Lord as we headed up the mountain to Shepherd's Inn.

Once we checked into our room, anxiety hit me. The room was nice and peaceful and contained no distractions, such as a television. But my thoughts were deafening. However, I still managed to rest with my wife until dinner. After eating, we walked out on the huge balcony that overlooks the chapel and the trees below. I could see the steeple emerging through the trees. We decided to walk down to the chapel and look around before the service started that evening.

It felt surreal for me to be standing in the same chapel where Billy Graham preached. I realized that I would soon be ordained as a deacon of Christ right there. The pastor had decided to start the spiritual retreat with my ordination, which was fine with me. I was ready and qualified. Jesus said, "…If ye continue in my word, then are ye my disciples indeed; And ye shall know the truth, and the truth shall make you free." (John 8:31-32)

As the time got closer, more and more people arrived at the chapel. Soon, the service was starting and I was being called up to the front. I do not remember much of the ordination service. All I do remember was standing there, with two ministers praying for me to receive the anointing of the Holy Spirit. I received it and then walked back to my seat while everyone started to praise and worship God. My wife hugged and congratulated me and things started to come back into focus during praise and worship time.

As I joined in, I audibly heard the Lord God say to me, "You have been released." I looked behind me to see if he was standing there; the voice had been so strong. However, I only saw two women, standing there with their hands lifted up. I said, "Thank you, Lord, for the release." I smiled and turned to my wife, who was singing. I told her that the Lord had released us from debt. She smiled and went back to singing. I knew she didn't really understand what I meant.

I was so pleased with the message. I could have grabbed my wife by the hand, walked out of the service, and packed up our bags to travel home. I had received what I had come for--what a blessing! And the retreat had just started. However, I stayed for the additional blessings and enjoyed myself. The staff was warm and friendly, the grounds and facilities were immaculate, the food was delicious, and I felt the presence of God throughout the entire place.

I did not tell anyone but my wife that I heard the Lord audibly speak to me because they would have not believed me. It took my wife about six months to fully understand what I had told her. I had to demonstrate it to her. That is when I received the revelation that, "...the kingdom of God is not in word, but in power." (1 Cor. 4:20). At this point, I realized I would need to demonstrate to everyone I came in contact with how the kingdom of God works. This is for the edification and spiritual maturity in Christ for the perfecting of the saints.

"That we henceforth be no more children, tossed to and fro, and carried about with every wind of doctrine, by the sleight of men, and cunning craftiness, whereby they lie in wait to deceive; But speaking the truth in love, may grow up into him in all things, which is the head, even Christ...." (Eph. 4:14-15)

The lesson in the Lord's school is all about being renewed in our spirits and in our minds. If you have not learned about Christ, you will be deceived by the doctrine of men. I received the teaching of the Holy Spirit, which says we are to compare spiritual truth against things that appear spiritual. The Lord led me to this verse: "But the natural man receiveth not the things of the Spirit of God: for they are foolishness unto him: neither can he know them, because they are spiritually discerned." (1 Cor. 2:14)

I had proof that the Lord God allowed me to graduate from the wisdom of man and the things of this world. He brought me to a deeper truth: that I do not know anything without prayer. I did not have the gift of eloquence. I did not speak with enticing words from the wisdom of man. But I was able to speak of what the Spirit, power, and might had done in my life. The deeper truth for the mature is this: "That your faith should not stand in the wisdom of men, but in the power of God." (1 Cor. 2:5)

The believer's walk must be trod by faith, not by sight. I was willing to be absent from my body and trust in the Lord. This was in readiness for death, so that whether I was present or absent, I could be accepted by him. But in order to be present with the Lord and for him to make his abode in me, I had to separate myself from evil associations.

Once I came down off that mountaintop and back into the valley, I had to clean up my material life. The Lord began purging me of all the clutter that existed in my house. I threw away hundreds of old CD's, spare pots and pans, plastic cups and plates, alcohol, unused toys, old medicine, expired food and spices, old socks and underwear, excess furniture, pictures, old rugs, and more. I searched the house, on a mission of order and cleanliness. If it was old, I threw it out!

I felt the Lord saying to me: "Having therefore these promises, dearly beloved, let us cleanse ourselves from all filthiness of the flesh and spirit, perfecting holiness in the fear of God." (2 Cor. 7:1)

"Therefore if any man be in Christ, he is a new creature: old things are passed away; behold, all things are become new." (2 Cor. 5:17)

God and I had reconciled and he called me totally and

unreservedly to himself. He made me an ambassador at large; a plenipotentiary with full power for Christ. I was an overlord, if you will. I had received the Spirit. I now had full power to transact business on behalf of the kingdom of heaven on earth and I received this privilege gladly and willingly.

I felt Jesus telling me, "…My kingdom is not of this world…." (John. 18:36). I was overwhelmed by the revelation that I was operating in the wrong kingdom; I was in the world's kingdom and not God's. This was why I had not prospered financially. I had not made God the Father my only God. I had others, such as the god of credit cards and the god of loans.

The Lord God advised me to leave behind man's way of doing things and to trust in the Father. This would be my only source of blessings. I came out of the old self that same day. I did not run or jog; I walked out, without fear. The material things of this world did not matter to me. I had shown this by my detachment to the old things I had accumulated. Amen.

I cut up my credit cards and mailed them back to the companies. I asked the Lord to forgive me for my debt and forgive my debtors for putting me in captivity.

If you are a believer in Christ Jesus and you are in debt, living from paycheck to paycheck, or lacking the finances to pay your bill, you must change your thinking. Abandon your worldly mindset that these cares have nothing to do with the kingdom of God. Come out of the world's system of debt today! If you are a believer working a full-time job and you are not able to save at least ten percent of your income, you are living above your means and need to make changes in how you spend your money.

When I made the Lord God my only source of financial

blessings, my mindset changed to the kingdom's way. I began trusting in the Lord to provide whatever I needed, when I needed it. He said that he would give me whatever I needed, according to his riches in glory, and so I tested the Spirit.

First, I asked him for peace. The Lord released me from debt and he also showed me the easy way out: the way of the cross. It was time to carry my cross and follow him. I cannot be in prayer with the Prince of Peace and not feel that peace within my spirit. Following the Holy Spirit is having a life filled with peace. Being in debt is not peaceful; it brings turmoil. So I paid off my debt immediately, instead of doing it halfway with a nickel-and-dime approach. That is the way of the world. No sir, that was not for me!

Secondly, I asked the Lord for joy. He sent two of my co-workers to be managers at two different companies. One of them offered me a job that had a significantly higher salary and a monthly bonus. I accepted! Six months later, the Holy Spirit moved the other former co-worker to offer me a job making even more money than I was making at my current job. I accepted and went to work for him.

Finally, I asked the Lord for love. He instructed me to begin serving my wife and kids. For example, instead of having my wife cook after a hard day's work, I would take them out to dinner. The Lord taught me to help clean our house without complaining. It bothered me that the children left things laying around, put things where they didn't belong, or left their rooms messy. With the help of the Holy Spirit, I stopped complaining and began quietly cleaning up the messes. This in itself was a better witness to the power of the Holy Spirit working in my life than if I had used one hundred words.

I would straighten up my wife's side of the closet, make all the beds, vacuum the floors and wash the clothes; in other words, do whatever need to be done. I began to enjoy organizing the house. There was no way I was going to let my wife out serve me. By doing all these things, my wife no longer made excuses about housework: there wasn't any! Little did I realize that the Lord had made me a servant so that I might show his love for others.

I had asked the Lord God for peace, joy, and love. He, in turn, radically changed my life. I did not pray for a financial blessing; I did not pray for a job; I did not pray that the Lord would change my family. I started to prosper in every area of my life when I decided to trust in God's way of doing things instead of the world's way of doing things.

The more I operated under faith, the more the Lord God revealed. The more the Lord God revealed, the more I realized I had not been living my life as a true Christian. As my thinking changed, I found myself wanting to encourage others to strive for a higher standard. This was a major revelation to me. I had thought I was living a Christian life, while instead I was in bondage. Yet the more I encouraged other to strive for a higher standard, the more I was rejected. I started to lose friends.

The Lord God tried to console me by explaining that they were not rejecting me, they were rejecting him. That was disheartening. How can Christians reject the truth? Apparently, it was easy because they were not true believers. They didn't have faith. They didn't rely on God. Many Christians are walking in head knowledge and not heart knowledge (faith). I knew this first-hand because I had experienced it myself.

Once the Lord God purged me from the world's way of doing things and renewed my mind to the way of the kingdom, he revealed the unexpected. Many pastors, bishops, and apostles were not walking in the way of the kingdom. They were trusting in the world's way and I could see this by their fruit—many had personal debt and even worse, had plunged their own churches into debt.

So they stayed at the level of man with limitations instead of at the level of God without limitations. The level of faith that I experienced had no limitations. Most of the pastors, bishops, and apostles were borrowers, and servants to the lenders, because of the vast amount of debt they had accumulated. It began to bother me because the people were duped into believing that the leaders of the churches were doing the right thing with their money. However, many leaders were using the money for their own selfish gain.

The more the Lord God revealed to me, the more I realized that this was completely out of control. Many pastors knew that they were wrong, but because they were in so much personal and church debt they could not, or would not, repent of this mismanagement of the tithes and offering. In some instances, it became so rampant that several of the pastors' homes and churches were in foreclosure, and yet they were still encouraging the people to pay the ten percent tithe.

Because of this, the Holy Spirit, my most invaluable teacher, led me to study everything in the Bible about tithing so that I would know the truth. Everything that I previously known about tithing came from what I was taught by the pastors and in reading or discussing it with other people. So I began to study directly from the source, the Bible. I soon realized everything that I had been taught was a false interpretation of biblical truth. It had been distorted by men. They had turned a community of believers' time of thanksgiving and rejoicing into a focus of the all mighty dollar bill.

After my in-depth study of the biblical truth about tithing,

I wrote my first book, Tithing: You Don't Have to Pay to Give. This book was in direct opposition to what pastors everywhere are preaching: that in order to be blessed and to prosper in this world, you have to pay a ten percent tithe to the church. For years, I paid tithes and I did not prosper. One of the reasons for this is that the church operates under the world's system and is in debt. This is not what the kingdom of God teaches; no one pays money in the kingdom of heaven. Faith is the currency there, not money.

The world system of debt is not designed for me to prosper. The world's system is designed for only one thing, and that is to keep me paying. The church is in debt to the world's system and it needs my money to pay its bills. A major part of being a deacon of Christ is helping God's people to become believers. I continued to share the truth of the kingdom of heaven with everyone who would listen until it came time for me to graduate from that church.

The Lord God corrected me when I realized I had been relying upon the teachings of man, instead of delving into the Word for myself and asking the Holy Spirit for guidance. He had me focus on the Spirit of God and not the spirit of man. In this way, I realized that the Holy Spirit is my most invaluable teacher. Ever since that day, I've trusted and believed only what the Holy Spirit said to me.

I attended my church for three and a half years. On the seventh day of the eighth month in the year 2006, I graduated from church school. I folded up my append-a-flex folder with acco fasteners and walked out of class. Thank you, Holy Spirit, for my degree. Hallelujah!

That day was one of the most memorable days of my life. It was so surreal. I had regained control of my life and I had stepped out of the world's way and the church's way of doing things. I was trusting solely in the Holy Spirit. To me, it was the death of preaching. I had completed sixteen years of grade school and sixteen years of church school. A valuable life lesson I had was this: "…godliness with contentment is great gain." (1 Tim. 6:6).

"Not that I speak in respect of want: for I have learned, in whatsoever state I am, therewith to be content." (Phil. 4:11)

Let's have a moment of silence…

GRADUATING FROM CHURCH SCHOOL

Part 3

10

As a father of two daughters, and "…because ye have known him that is from the beginning…" (1 John 2:13), my focus shifted solely to the spiritual things: love, joy, peace, longsuffering, gentleness, goodness, faith, meekness, and temperance. Against such, there is no law. I stopped thinking that I must attend church school every Sunday and pay tithes in order to find favor with the Lord. Jesus walked by the fruits of the Spirit and he knew there wasn't anything the law could bring against him for showing the love of the Father to his people. He knew that the only way the lawgivers could accuse him was falsely.

Spiritually, I had received my degree for passing the test that the Lord God set before me: I had mastered my faith in him. God my

Father wanted me to get past the point where I felt as though I had to go to a church building for the teaching and doctrines of Christ. This is when the Holy Spirit became so important to me.

I used this revelation, meditating on the things of the Father and applying them to my life as a father. The more I meditated on being a father to my children, the more I realized that God our Father was dealing with the same things that I had to deal with as a father.

As a father, it is my job to teach my children, and someday my children's children, about how this world works using a biblical kingdom prospective. It is my job to help my family understand how I defeated the tyranny of this world system and to make sure they know that I will defend them at all cost. As a parent, I am to lay down my life for future generations. I am the example of liberty for them. It is my responsibility to train up my children in the way that they should go because eventually, they will graduate and go into the world themselves.

When my daughters were young, my wife and I watched them grow and develop. We knew their strengths and weaknesses, so we focused on enhancing those strengths and developing the weaknesses. My wife and I notice that our girls were visual learners at an early age.

In order to help them to develop, we took them to a professional learning center to have them tested. The results came back that they were high level, visual learners. This meant they preferred having pictures while reading and got bored quickly with text-only books. Reading can be stressful to a visual learner. The shorter the articles are, the better.

I noticed that if I gave my younger daughter, Sydney, a magazine on dogs, she could tell me about every dog in there. So I subscribed to a magazine in her name and now she recognizes almost every dog she sees. If I bought my oldest daughter, Lamari, a magazine about a famous person of interest, she could recount much about the topic. We used these magazines to encourage our daughters to read more.

Jesus said, "Have faith in God." (Mark 11:22) Faith comes by hearing the word of God and believing by faith that God is God. As a believer, I must walk by faith and not by sight. I must believe what the Lord God says and not what the devil says. In this world, we use words. Words may not be adequate to discuss God—but it is all we have. So I had to learn to tame my tongue and be vigilant over the words I used. I needed to listen and do what his Word commanded. Then, at some point, I could just "be."

We are such a culture of doers. If we are not doing something, we are listening to the radio, watching television, staring at a computer screen, or glued to the handheld devices that keep us captive 24/7. We have lost the sense of reverence that comes of "being" with God.

As a father, I have learned that most people are, "Ever learning, and never able to come to the knowledge of the truth." (2 Tim. 3:7) People love to learn, but most of them never put into practice what they have learned. The knowledge of the truth is not the real problem; the true dilemma lies in applying knowledge to life in a meaningful way. This requires real change.

I came up with a way to apply what I had learned to my life. First of all, I thanked the Lord God for the prophetic process that he took me through in order to become a true believer. As a believer in Christ and the way of the kingdom, I had to get to the point where I trusted the Lord God whole heartedly to show me his ways, teach me his paths, and lead me in his truth. Once I understood who I was in Christ, it was easy to graduate from church school and begin walking my life path by faith.

I had no idea that life after graduation from church school would be so awesome. I did not miss the struggles associated with church, such as waking up early. I no longer had to deal with pastors who preached without a biblical basis; appeals for money that caused debt on the part of the church or was tied into a false promise of riches; claims of a curse-with-a-curse; prayer meetings; mid-week Bible studies; choir practices; and so on. Thank you, Jesus, for graduating me.

I am not saying that I will never visit a church again; I go from time to time. But I am an alumnus of the institutional church. I do not need to be a member of a church building to have a funeral and to be buried. The only spiritual father I need is God, who is the only spiritual Father there is. Many of the so-called apostles, prophets, evangelists, pastors, and teachers that I have met are often too far removed from God the Father to be able to help those seeking the kingdom of God. Many people attending church are sincere in their desire to follow God's will for their lives. However, the lost cannot lead the lost.

Christ is my spiritual head and he should be yours as well. Have you not read that Christ is, "Far above all principality, and power, and might, and dominion, and every name that is named, not only in this world, but also in that which is to come: And hath put all things under his feet, and gave him to be the head over all things to the church, Which is his body, the fullness of him that filleth all in all." (Eph. 1:21-23)

Christ is the head; we are the body, which means your pastor is also a part of the body. There is only one head to a body. Feet are attached to the body and the devil is beneath the feet. So if I am in the body of Christ, the devil is under my feet.

Many Christians try to make people feel guilty about not going to church. Unfortunately, many of them are hypocrites or pretenders, just as I was. I have stopped asking people if they are Christians. My question has changed to, "Are you a believer?" A lot of people know Christ, but do not believe in him. My daughters know that I love them, but do they really believe that I love them? A policeman know that a bullet proof vest will save his life, but does he believe it enough to put one on every day?

You may not recognize the difference between a Christian and a believer. Some Christians still do things the world's way, whereas believers do things God's way. You will never know where you belong unless you take a step back and examine your life through the eyes of the Holy Spirit. Ideally, this is what a good pastor and church do for you: encourage and stretch you outside of your comfort zone. However, you still need to know the Word of God, be filled with the Holy Spirit, and not only understand, but do what Christ Jesus asks of you in order to become a true believer. No amount of talking, preaching, classes, or activities can get us to that level; only a true faith in God. Every time I consider the revelation the Lord gave me about graduating from church school, I praise him. This is by far one of the greatest revelations I have received and it has strengthened my relationship with the Father. It is obvious why. There is no one else to go to, only the Father. My trust, my love, and my loyalty rest only in him.

After graduating from church school, I reflected back on all the years of searching, being confused by false teachings, and the errors in my belief system. I knew this was the process I needed to go through in order to reach the place that I am in today. I repented to the Lord God for not studying harder. I should have graduated years ago. I spent too much time on religion, listening to storyteller after storyteller. I have to admit that I had a Word deficiency, meaning I had an insufficiency in understanding the Bible. In this state of mind, I was inadequately armed to combat wrong teachings. I had no way of realizing that I was outside the realm of the kingdom of God.

Religion appears to love God, love the church, love the pastor, love the kids, and be hardworking, shouting praise, volunteering, tithing, ushering, and being involved in activity after activity. None of this is bad in and of itself. But this is far from following the straight and narrow path. All those things don't bring you to salvation. In the religious mindset, a person is devoted to religion instead of seeking godliness.

Do not confuse activity with results. Religious people are busy doing a lot of activities, but they go into church one way and leave the same way: unchanged and without results. Remember Big Tex! It's time to graduate from religion.

We all need to begin somewhere. Nobody can expect to graduate without some preparation. In fact, my story may not be your story at all. You may decide that church is exactly where you want to remain and that is fine. As long as you are grounded in the Word and have a relationship with the Holy Spirit, he will lead you exactly where you need to go.

Here is what I've discovered after years of church attendance. Most people get stuck because their pastor spends his Sundays reading his notes to the congregation or he follows a Scripture reading with a story.

Grade teachers tell stories to children all the time. I do not expect a child to walk before she crawls, so why would I expect a child to read and write before she can hold a pencil, make controlled marks, or recognize her name? If an educator is going to teach at a primary level, the curriculum must be based on sound child development principles and meet the specific needs of the child.

Examine your pastor's style of preaching. Does he read his notes to the congregation and tell stories after reading only one or two passages from Scripture? Think about how a grade school teacher reads to her students from the teacher's handbook and uses stories as an example to get her point across. Both styles are very similar. You will have to graduate from this style of teaching if you plan to mature spiritually in Christ.

11

DEACON OF CHRIST: FRANKLIN

I continue to be a servant of Jesus Christ to everyone that has obtained faith through the righteousness of God and our Savior, Jesus Christ. I pray that grace and peace be with you through the knowledge of the Lord God. I pray that you receive godliness and an understanding of the Divine Power. Godliness is the goal that we are pressing towards.

Paul said, "For bodily exercise profiteth little: but godliness is profitable unto all things…." (1 Tim. 4:8) The purpose of our lives is to walk every day in the character of the Lord God.

Peter said, "…giving all diligence, add to your faith virtue;

and to virtue knowledge; And to knowledge temperance; and to temperance patience; and to patience godliness; And to godliness brotherly kindness; and to brotherly kindness charity. For if these things be in you, and abound, they make you that ye shall neither be barren nor unfruitful in the knowledge of our Lord Jesus Christ. But he that lacketh these things is blind, and cannot see afar off, and hath forgotten that he was purged from his old sins. Wherefore the rather, brethren, give diligence to make your calling and election sure: for if ye do these things, ye shall never fall...." (2 Pet. 1:5-10)

James said, "Confess your faults (not your sins) one to another, and pray one for another, that ye may be healed. The effectual fervent prayer of a righteous man availeth much." (James 5:16)

John said, "And this is the promise that he hath promised us, even eternal life. These things have I written unto you concerning them that seduce you. But the anointing which ye have received of him abideth in you, and ye need not that any man teach you: but as the same anointing teacheth you of all things, and is truth, and is no lie, and even as it hath taught you, ye shall abide in him. And now, little children, abide in him; that, when he shall appear, we may have confidence, and not be ashamed before him at his coming. If ye know that he is righteous, ye know that every one that doeth righteousness is born of him." (1 John 2:25-29)

The Lord God is trying to get us back to the point where Adam was before sin. Jesus is the standard; our goal is to be like Christ Jesus, not Abraham, David, Moses, or Elijah. God corrected Peter immediately on the Mount of Transfiguration when he tried to put Elijah and Moses on the same level with Jesus.

Peter said to Jesus, "...Lord, it is good for us to be here: if thou wilt, let us make here three tabernacles; one for thee, and one for

Moses, and one for Elias. While he yet spake, behold, a bright cloud overshadowed them: and behold a voice out of the cloud, which said, This is my beloved Son, in whom I am well pleased; hear ye him. And when the disciples heard it, they fell on their face, and were sore afraid. And Jesus came and touched them, and said, Arise, and be not afraid. And when they had lifted up their eyes, they saw no man, save Jesus only." (Matt. 17:4-8)

God is saying that Moses represented the law and it has been replaced; Elijah represented the prophets and they have been replaced. Moses led the people out of Egypt, yet even he did not enter the promised land. Elijah entered heaven bodily, as a precursor to Christ, because he was a faithful servant. However, we are to hear and follow only Jesus.

I learned by studying the Scriptures. By reading about the disciples of Jesus, I learned what it means to be a deacon. You can learn how to better serve the Lord by reading about those who served him first. In the Scriptures, we have example after example of how man fails God. Yet God's love for man still does not change. I learned the right and wrong way of doing things by reading about Moses, Elijah, and the other prophets.

Peter was sinful, prideful, and even denied knowing the Lord. But through his example, we know that he was repentant and the Lord forgave him. This is unlike Judas Iscariot, who was so upset by his own actions that he took his own life. If he had been repentant, the Lord would have forgiven him as well. The Lord is patient with us.

James failed when he fell asleep with the others in the garden. He could not even wait with Jesus for one hour in prayer. John, known to us as the beloved disciple, was left in charge of

Mary, the mother of Jesus, at the foot of the cross. Jesus knew that John exemplified love and that he would care for Mary in Jesus' absence.

In a journey of perseverance, Jesus took his disciples up the mountain to withstand the elements not only bodily, but spiritually. It was on the mountaintop that Jesus revealed to the disciples that he was truly God. These are the things that the Scriptures revealed to me in my studies.

Jesus came to save us. He walked this earth to give us a glimpse of how Adam walked with God before he sinned. How wonderful that is! No matter what, if you establish yourself in Christ, no man or devil can deceive you. You cannot be misled in Christ; you cannot fall in Christ. If you are being deceived, you are not in union with Christ because that would mean that Christ can be deceived. Won't you allow Abba Father to love you? You cannot give up something for Christ's sake and not believe he will bless you.

Listen to me now, believe me later on…

The young prophets built their houses by the River Jordan because it was the position of transition. I cannot be stuck out of position when God wants me to transition. So I have to stay ready until it is time. It is the way of the cross.

Everything came into existence because of the spoken word of God. The Lord God never did anything without speaking it first. That is why we never do anything without speaking it first. My heart is the center of my life and it should be carefully guarded because it is the source of faith and can be subject to evil. Whatever is in abundance in the heart, the mouth will speak.

Everything after Genesis, chapter 3, is a fallen concept. It was then that humanity put limitations around itself. It was Jesus who put us back in our rightful place, with the Father in our minds. We must be spiritual men and not natural, or worldly, men. In God's class, there are no limitations. Satan wanted to keep me boxed up in a church building, but he could not contain a free man. I had to get my spirit, soul, and body to become one. Once that happened, it was a wrap.

12

The Lord God gave me a vision. I had a dream where I met two young guys outside of a museum. One of the guys was black with reddish brown hair and the other guy had black hair and was Indian. I briefly spoke to them and then went on my way. As I stood outside of the museum, a twister, like a dust devil, sprang up suddenly. I saw it spinning paper through the trees in the forest. It appeared to be walking through the trees. I shouted to everyone to go inside the museum because it was going to turn and come our way. Everyone ran into the museum except one woman, who seemed to be in shock and could not move. I grabbed the woman and pulled her inside. We could hear the twister on top of the building, but suddenly, it left.

As I walked through the museum, I looked over the second floor railing to see a crowd staring at a Nephilim that was about fifty feet tall. He was sitting on the floor, chained up by the wrists and ankles. He was giant; about the size of King Kong. He was sitting there, looking very angry. I ran to escape from him because I knew those chains could not hold him for long.

I could hardly believe I was getting the chance to see an actual giant. I had been telling people that there were giants in the days of old, but no one believed me. God had pointed out to me in several places in the Bible where the giants dwelled.

"There were giants in the earth in those days; and also after that, when the sons of God came in unto the daughters of men, and they bare children to them, the same became mighty men which were of old, men of renown." (Gen. 6:4)

Go-li'ath, the Philistine from Gath, was a descendent of the giants.

"And they brought up an evil report of the land which they had searched unto the children of Israel, saying, The land, through which we have gone to search it, is a land that eateth up the inhabitants thereof; and all the people that we saw in it are men of a great stature. And there we saw the giants, the sons of Anak, which come of the giants: and we were in our own sight as grasshoppers, and so we were in their sight." (Num. 13:32-33)

The Nephilims were so big that they could step on a person as if he was a grasshopper. The E'mims and the An'a-kims were also giants.

"The E'mims dwelt therein in times past, a people great, and many, and tall, as the An'a-kims; Which also were accounted giants, as The An'a-kims; but the Moabites called them E'mims." (Deut. 2:10-11)

The giants that dwelt in Ar, on the coast of Moab were called the Zam-zum-mims. "That also was accounted a land of giants: giants dwelt therein in old time; and the Ammon-ites call them Zam-zum-mims; A people great, and many, and tall, as the An'a-kims;" (Deut. 2:18-21)

There were even giants in the land of Per'-iz-zites.

"And Josh'u-a answered them, If thou be a great people, then get thee up to the wood country, and cut down for thyself there in the land of the Per'-iz-zites and of the giants, if mount E'phra-im be too narrow for thee." (Josh. 17:5)

"A whole valley of giants lived on the north of Hin'nom." (Josh. 18:16)

Now back to the dream…

WOW! So as I quickly moved to get away from the giant, I

heard chaos behind me. The giant had stood up, breaking the chains with his hands, and was wreaking havoc in the building. He was destroying everything and it seemed as though everywhere I tried to hide, he found me. He was getting closer and closer. I figured that the only way to escape this giant was to get out of the building.

I located an opening and ran for the exit. Once outside, I hid underneath some shrubbery with some other people who were already hiding there, but I still did not feel safe. So I ran farther back into the woods and hid behind a large tree with two other people. I saw others hiding behind trees. They tried to convince me that we were safe, but I still did not feel safe.

As I looked around for somewhere else to hide, I saw a light shining at me in the distance, as though someone was signaling me to come, but I could not see anyone that far away. Having no fear, I ran deeper into the woods towards the spot where I saw the light. The people hiding behind the trees were yelling at me, trying to convince me not to go, but I did not listen and they did not follow me. When I finally reached the spot where the light originated, there were people waiting to help me escape from the giant.

What I saw at this point was incredible and words cannot do it justice. It was as if the tree of life had transcended time. I thought to myself, surely this tree has been here since the beginning of time. The tree was so massive that people were walking around inside it. As the people directed me to climb up inside the tree, I did so without hesitation, ascending the tree. I did not look back and I did not stop. I just followed the people walking ahead of me. The climb was similar to climbing steps, but in some spots, I had to use my hands to pull myself up higher.

As we went high and higher, I noticed people along the way who were just standing and talking. Some were sitting. We did not stop to talk to anyone, we just kept moving forward. It seemed like we walked up that tree for miles and miles without becoming tired. We came to a point that flattened out and we walked straight ahead. I noticed that some of the people ahead of me had disappeared.

As we continued to walk, we passed through a section where people were lying everywhere asleep. There were so many people that it appeared that they were sleeping on top of each other. We literally had to walk over them because they were sleeping on the pathway. Stepping on people did not bother the three people ahead of me. They just walked on them like it was very normal, but I was very nervous that someone would wake up and be mad at me for stepping on them. No one woke up and I never stopped walking.

After we cleared this area, we came to another section that was filled with babies wrapped up in blue and white blankets. There were crying bundles everywhere. They were all over the pathway and again, we had to walk through them to continue on the path. I tried my best not to step on the babies, but it was really difficult not to. The three people ahead of me had no problem stepping on the babies because they were not hurting them. I was afraid that I was going to hurt one of them, but I did not. And so I continued on my path, not looking back or stopping.

All of a sudden, something even stranger happened. A two-car supersonic train pulled up, dropped off a load of babies, and jetted off. It was so weird. I watched as some ladies quickly wrapped the babies in blankets and placed them alongside the ones in blue and white blankets. At this point, I was thinking that I was going to run into a huge pregnant woman having babies, but thank God I did not.

As I continued on the path of babies, I noticed that there were only two men ahead of me now. During the distractions in the baby section, one of them had disappeared. Nevertheless, I continued on the path without looking back and without stopping. After, we had made it through the section with crying babies, we came to another section we needed to cross. Here, people were lying around sleeping again. I thought to myself, you have to be kidding me. What in the world is going on with all these people?

It was at this point that the two guys ahead of me stopped, stepped aside, and let me continue on the path. I walked through the crowd of sleeping people with no problems; I didn't wake up a single person. Wow! It started to get a little darker and then all of a sudden, I broke through a veil into the daylight.

It was an awesome sight to see the daylight. Once I was out, the first person that I saw was the black guy with reddish brown hair that I had encountered at the beginning of my dream. He was much older now and his hair was long, with a long reddish brown beard to match. I was so happy to see someone I knew. I ran up to give him a hug. He welcomed me and invited me to his house. As we walked there, I noticed the king and queen of the tribe sitting there, smiling at the children as they played. When we arrived at my friend's house, his wife prepared us food to eat. It was then that I woke up.

As I meditated on this bizarre dream, I wondered how it was significant to me and my spiritual walk. I believe if you trust the Lord God with all your heart and have no fear, he will make a way of escape for you. Through the believer's walk of faith, God's blessing will endure from generation to generation. The people that were on the path represented three generations and the people I saw once I came out represented the fourth generation. I was able to go forward in time and walk through four generations of people.

Have faith in the Lord God…

13

"People often say that motivation doesn't last long. Well, neither does bathing – that's why we recommend it daily." Zig Ziglar

The following topics are some of my meditations.

THE LORD GOD

The reason why I dedicated this book to the Lord God is because of the revelations I received while studying the book of Genesis.

I noticed in Genesis, chapter one, that it says, God created, God moved, God said, God saw, God divided, God called, God, God, God.... In chapter one, it is Elohim who is doing this. Elohim is God, our creator.

Then I noticed in chapter two how the Lord God was introduced. The Lord God made, the Lord God had, the Lord God formed, the Lord God planted, the Lord God took, the Lord God, the Lord God, the Lord God.... In chapter two, it is Yahweh doing this. Yahweh is God's name.

As I continued reading Genesis, chapter three, I read that it was the Lord God, Yahweh, who created the serpent. But the serpent did not say unto the woman, "Yea, hath the Lord God said, ye shall not eat of every tree of the garden?" The serpent merely said, "Hath God said...." He did not acknowledge the Lord.

When using words, you must be careful about just saying God instead of Jesus, the Lord God. When you say the Lord God, you are acknowledging Jesus Christ. Don't be like the serpent and conveniently omit Jesus Christ, the Lord God, in your conversations with people who do not believe that Jesus Christ is the Messiah, the Son of the Living God.

Many in the church are in an infant state. It's not that they cannot eat on their own, they are just lazy. This should be a charge to us all to grow up, look at the Word, and be open to God's leadings.

TEST OUT

In my current job, I have to periodically complete on-line training classes. But if I have already taken the classes before, I do not have to read through the whole session again. I can just test out of the class. Normally, a session takes about an hour and a half to complete. If I test out, I can skip the reading session and go straight to the test. It only takes about thirty minutes to test out. The test materials are the same, year after year, with a little variation.

In a similar way, I had to graduate from the church test. Year after year, I had sat in a pew, not learning anything. I had to test out and be finished with the class (the church).

I thank you, God, for maturing me.

"Thy word is a lamp unto my feet, and a light unto my path." (Ps. 119:105)

"The entrance of thy words giveth light; it giveth understanding unto the simple." (Ps.119:130)

The Word of our Father lives and he wants us to know it in its simplicity. We just have to take the time to read it and live.

"The righteousness of thy testimonies is everlasting: give me understanding, and I shall live." (Ps. 119:144)

VISITATIONS BY THE HOLY SPIRIT

The Holy Spirit woke me up early one morning, around three o'clock, and said in a small, still voice, "Franklin, get up, man.

I have something to show you in Colossians." He did not tell me where in Colossians. So I got up and read the whole book of Colossians. The next morning, the same thing happened, but this time his instructions were different.

"Franklin, get up, man. I have something to show you in Galatians."

But he would not tell me where in Galatians. So I got up and read the whole book of Galatians. The next night it was Ephesians, then Philippians, Thessalonians, Titus, Philemon, Hebrews, Timothy, James, Peter, John, Jude, and lastly, I read Revelation. It was then that he let me rest.

THE GOD CLASS

I'm in God's class.

Tip your brass,

No drinking out of glass,

I told you.

I was in God's class.

"Far above all principality, and power, and might, and dominion, and every name that is named, not only in this world, but also in that which is to come...." (Eph. 1:21)

A DISABILITY SERVICE

To assist people who are spiritually deaf, hard of hearing, or have speech disabilities, we accept RELAY calls for assistance.

THE STRONGHOLD OF THE FAMILY CHURCH

A family church is a church that most of the family members attend. The stronghold of some family churches has been to keep generations in an immature state of mind in Christ. This stronghold has held some people in bondage to religion their whole lives. There are some people in the family church that have never experienced that true, spiritual side of God.

ECCLESIA

"Ecclesia" refers to church or to those who have been called out. Israel was called out of Egypt and she is spoken of as an assembly, or an ecclesia, in the wilderness. In no sense was Israel a New Testament church, except as a foreshadowing of that which was to come. Ecclesia is applied to a body of professed believers in Christ.

JONAH

I received a revelation while meditating on Jonah getting swallowed up by a giant fish.

"Now the Lord had prepared a great fish to swallow up Jonah...." (Jon. 1:17) [Comment: the Lord has "a prepared place" for his hard-headed children. God will watch over his Word with divine care, preservation, and mercy. The Lord's Word will not return to him void. It will accomplish what he pleases.]

"...And Jonah was in the belly of the fish three days and three nights." (Jon. 1:17) [Comment: you have three days and three nights to be delivered from the imprisonment of death, hell, and the grave. Deliverance and salvation is of the Lord. Repent and live.]

"Then Jonah prayed unto the Lord his God out of the fish's belly. And said, I cried by reason of mine affliction unto the Lord, and he heard me; out of the belly of hell cried I, and thou heardest my voice." (Jon. 2:1-2)

"When my soul fainted within me I remembered the Lord: and my prayer came in unto thee, into thine holy temple. They that observe lying vanities forsake their own mercy. But I will sacrifice unto thee with the voice of thanksgiving; I will pay that that I have vowed. Salvation is of the Lord. And the Lord spake unto the fish, and it vomited out Jonah upon the dry land." (Jon. 2:7-10)

GAMALIEL'S ADVICE

Take heed: be careful whom you lay hands on. The apostles Peter and John were arrested for healing the man who was lame from birth. He had lain by the gate every day, calling out to the beautiful and people who had started following the disciples.

"Then the high priest rose up, and all they that were with him, (which is the sect of the Sadducees,) and were filled with indignation, And laid their hands on the apostles, and put them in the common prison. But the angel of the Lord by night opened the prison doors, and brought them forth, and said, Go, stand and speak in the temple to the people all the words of this life. And when they heard that, they entered into the temple early in the morning, and taught. But the high priest came, and they that were with him, and called the council together, and all the senate of the children of Israel, and sent to the prison to have them brought." (Acts 5:17-21)

While in court, one of the councilmen named Gamaliel, a Pharisee and a doctor of the law, stood up and said to the high priest and the men of Israel, "…take heed to yourselves what ye intend to do as touching these men." (Acts. 5:35) Gamaliel's advice to the Sanhedrin was basically this: if the work of these men be of men, it will come to nothing, but if the work is of God, it is unstoppable!

Gamaliel reminded the people of Israel how, in times past, Theudas came boasting that he was somebody and people joined in with him. He was slain and the people following him were scattered and brought to nothing. Judas of Galilee drew a lot of people, but he also perished and all the people with him were dispersed.

"But if it be of God, ye cannot overthrow it; lest haply ye be found even to fight against God. And to him they agreed: and when they had called the apostles, and beaten them, they commanded that they should not speak in the name of Jesus, and let them go." (Acts 5:39-40)

Take heed.

THE JUSTICE LEAGUE

Simeon and Levi, the sons of Jacob, were the heads of the justice league. Their sister, Dinah, by Jacob and Leah, was taken, seduced, and defiled by Shechem, the prince of the country. Shechem was the son of Hamor, the chief of the country at that time. Dinah was between the ages of thirteen and fifteen, which was the age of marriage. When Jacob found out that Shechem had defiled Dinah his daughter, he told his sons. Simeon and Levi refused to allow the prince to get away with it.

So the two of them took their swords and went boldly into the city, slew all the males, including Hamor and his son Shechem, and took Dinah out of Shechem's house. They ruined the city because of what the corrupt men had done in defiling their sister. And they refused to allow the prince to deal with their sister as a harlot.

Justice League.

RIGOR MORTIS

Your spirit can leave your body for three days and return on the fourth day before rigor mortis will set in. Jesus knew this because it had been done before.

Rigor mortis is post-mortem corporal rigidity and stiffness. Medical information shows that rigor mortis peaks between twenty-four to forty-eight hours. It disappears in the same way as it develops.

GROW UP

How long are you going to stay immature in Christ? When are you going to realize that there is more to Christ than going to church? We are sheep and Christ is the Good Shepherd. When have you ever seen a sheep carry around anything? Then why are you carrying around worry, anxiety, pain, sickness, disease, and all that mess? Cast ALL of your cares on Christ.

"The Lord is my shepherd; I shall not want. He maketh me to lie down in green pastures: he leadeth me beside the still waters. He restoreth my soul: he leadeth me in the paths of righteousness for his name's sake. Yea, though I walk through the valley of the shadow of death, I will fear no evil: for thou art with me; the rod and thy staff they comfort me. Thou preparest a table before me in the presence of mine enemies: thou anointest my head with oil; my cup runneth over. Surely goodness and mercy shall follow me all the days of my life: and I will dwell in the house of the Lord for ever." (Ps. 23:1-6)

FRANKIE APPLESEED

You do not plant seeds to grow seeds. You plant seeds to grow trees. Fruit seeds do not produce fruit. Fruit seeds produce trees. Trees may or may not produce fruit. A tree grown from seed may not be good; as a matter of fact, it may be terrible. A tree that is grown from a seed will not bear fruit for at least five years and it will only bear fruit on those limbs that originated five years ago.

I researched "planting apple seeds" and you can as well. See what you find. You will learn that it is a process for a full-grown tree to grow. While seeds are cheap, the fruit, such as apples, are expensive. You do not take your seeds and sow them in another man's yard or field. You sow them in your own yard. Has anyone ever given you seeds? I want the fruit, not the seeds. Some people eat the whole apple, including the seeds. I do not, because I want the fruit, not the seeds. Apple seeds do not produce apples. Apple seeds produce apple trees that may or may not produce fruit. All apple trees do not produce fruit.

All men are not seed producers. All women do not produce babies. There is good soil and bad soil. Some women have good soil, but are yoked with a man with no seed or bad seed. Some women who can have children want to have children, but they cannot because the man cannot.

The seed/child is in the man, but some women do not want the man. They just want the child in the man. The same goes for the church. Most of the church does not want Jesus; the church wants the things Jesus can do.

Jesus is the spouse. The husband is first. Submit yourself to your own husband. The child is second. Do not put your child before your husband.

What is causing the woman not to believe the Christ that is in her husband? The Christ in him cannot lie. The people that I want to know and love Christ the most are my wife and children. The enemy wants the wife to reject the husband's voice when he speaks about Christ, because he knows what happens when two or more come together in Christ. So satan tries to sow discord. He immediately tries to throw a gate up around the wife's heart when the Word of God is mentioned. But the gates of hell will not prevail. The enemy does not want the wife to receive the Christ in her husband; he wants her to be distracted by many things.

I pray that the Lord God gives me the wisdom to love my wife as a mature woman, and not as a young girl. Wives sometimes act like little girls when they do not get their way. Husbands, notice how you talk to your wives like daughters sometimes, instead of as full-grown women. Stop doing that! Pray for wisdom every day. Wisdom comes from the Lord. The same goes for men. Sometimes we pout if we don't get our way, just like little boys. We too must mature in Christ!

"And Jesus increased in wisdom and stature, and in favour with God and man." (Luke 2:52)

We have to pray daily that God increases our wisdom so we can mature in him. We should be a mature, loving husbands and wives together, on the same mission to grow closer to Christ. My prayer is for God to continue to grow me in the wisdom of the Lord. I pray the same for you as you communicate with your spouse. Amen.

NIC-O-LA'-I-TANES SYSTEM

"Nic-o" means to lord over. "La'-i-tanes" mean lay people. The word "Nic-o-la'-i-tanes" means to lord over the lay people. God disapproves of that. The Nic-o-la'-i-tanes were one of the sects which arose and plagued the church at Ephesus and Pergamos. They taught false doctrines, they denied the true faith, and became part of a group that upholds "the doctrine of Balaam." The only way to recognize false teaching is to be very familiar with the truth. You do this by studying and meditating on the Word of God.

Not "oh well" but "oh hell!" There is no need for the unbeliever to call a funeral home when the Lord God comes back. That consuming lake of fire will take care of all of his business.

My motivation is knowing what the Holy Spirit told me I could be.

YOKED!

A lot of pastors are unbelievers.

"Thou shalt not plow with an ox and an ass together." (Deut. 22:10)

Meaning, you cannot yoke a believer and an unbeliever together. While one is trying to plow ahead, the other one does not want to plow. If the ox tries to pull the donkey with that big strong neck, they are going to end up going in a circle. This is what is happening to many churches, as well as many marriages. They are going around in circles for years. If you are yoked up with an unbeliever, pray for him or her. There have been so many miracles of unbelieving spouses who have been saved by the prayers of their self-sacrificing and giving spouses.

FINANCIAL MANAGERS

Financial managers are preying on God's people. Kingdom citizens do not need a financial wellness coach. A financial wellness coach wants you to think that a house with a two-car garage, a Ferrari, an airplane, money, a great credit score, palm trees, and rental homes are the way to prosperity. They say that owning is everything.

Hold on, fathers, mother, sons, and daughters of God. We are heirs to the kingdom of God. We do not care about the worldly, material things that are going to pass away. We are to have faith in the Lord God and in his way of doing things. Why are you attending "Owning Everything Seminars" at a city near you, when the earth is the Lord's? Meditate on this: "But godliness with contentment is great gain." (1 Tim. 6:6) If you want to be rich and wealthy, all you have to do is be content in God, no matter what state you are in. We are just privileged to use his things while we are here. None of his stuff leaves the earth. All that stuff that King Tut had is still here.

"And Jesus answering saith unto them, Have faith in God. For verily I say unto you, That whosoever shall say unto this mountain, Be thou removed, and be thou cast into the sea; and shall not doubt in his heart, but shall believe that those things which he saith shall come to pass; he shall have whatsoever he saith." (Mark 11:22-23)

You need to use your faith to get the things in the world. The only fight we are supposed to be fighting is the good fight of faith.

It takes faith to save money. If you are not saving money, you are outside of the faith realm. It takes faith to not be in debt. If you are in debt, you are outside of the faith realm. If you are working every day, you are not broke because you do not have any money. You are broke because you do not have faith or you are stuck in a poverty mind set.

If you are able to make a three hundred dollar car payment for five years, you are able to save three hundred dollars for twenty-four months and then buy your car with cash. How is it that many say they can make a car payment for five years, but they cannot save money for twenty-four months? Elevate your thinking to God's way of doing things and be inside, instead of outside, the kingdom of God. If you save your money and purchase a car in cash, you eat from the fruit of peace, but if you take out a car loan for five years, you eat from the fruit of tribulation. But be of good cheer, because Christ has overcome the world.

"These things I have spoken unto you, that ye should not be offended." (John 16:1)

CUSSING AND FUSSING!

I have heard people say, "You need to go to church." But these same people are going to church and not learning a thing. So why would they want to send someone else to church?

Rather than sending someone to church, minister to them on the spot. You are the church. But if you are cussing and fussing like they are, how can you call yourself a child of God? I learned this revelation when it happened to me in my own life. Going down to the front of the church on Sunday and reciting Romans 10:9 does not make you a Christian. Being obedient to the Word of God, hearing and doing what the Holy Spirit directs you to do, and living a righteous life is what makes you a Christian.

I have heard that man is trying to be a spiritual covering. How is a carnal man going to be a spiritual father? There is only one father: God. He is the only Spiritual Father. Trust him only! Christ covers us, not man. There is only one way to the Father and that is through Christ Jesus. Get in Christ and the glory of the Lord will be revealed.

MARK OF FALSE TEACHERS

"Having eyes full of adultery, and that cannot cease from sin; beguiling unstable souls: an heart they have exercised with covetous practices; cursed children: Which have forsaken the right way, and are gone astray, following the way of Balaam the son of Bosor, who loved the wages of unrighteousness; But was rebuked for his iniquity: the dumb ass speaking with man's voice forbad the madness of the prophet. These are wells without water, clouds that are carried with a tempest; to whom the mist of darkness is reserved for ever." (2 Pet. 2:14-17)

SAND PILES

I received a vision one day while taking my daughter back to college from spring break. The vision looked a little something like this. My wife, my two daughters, and I were walking away from a church. I was walking slightly ahead of my wife, and my daughters were walking side by side slightly behind my wife. The four of us were looking forward. There was another man, about six paces behind my daughters, and he, his wife and daughter were looking back with half their bodies turning into sand. Behind them were another couple looking backward and half their bodies were turning into sand. After that, there were mounds of sand leading all the way back to the church doors.

My interpretation was this: once you graduate from church school, do not look back. Have faith and trust God.

SPIRITUAL INFANCY TO MATURITY

Just as an infant grows into a child, then a young adult, and ultimately, a full grown adult, he is guided, nurtured, and taught the way of life. Once he matures, he does not have to depend on his parents. He should be able to grasp life and move forward. This is the same for all church people. You have to develop through faith and not be dependent on others to forever teach you. You should mature so that you can lead another to Christ, and then that person can do the same in one long, unbroken chain.

IN CHRIST

When you are in Christ, you have access to the mind of Christ, the blood of Christ, the power of Christ, the love of Christ…I can go on and on. The Word of God says, "And I will give unto thee the keys of the kingdom of heaven: and whatsoever thou shalt bind on earth shall be bound in heaven: and whatsoever thou shalt loose on earth shall be loosed in heaven." (Matt. 16:19) Jesus did not say there is one key to the kingdom. He said there are many keys to the kingdom.

"And they overcame him by the blood of the Lamb, and by the word of their testimony...." (Rev. 12:11)

Our words are the most powerful things in the whole world.

"Grace be with you, mercy, and peace, from God the Father, and from the Lord Jesus Christ, the Son of the Father, in truth and love." (2 John 1:3)

The Lord God has made sure that we have everything we need to survive on the earth. Why are people not taking advantage?

MAMMON

Don't you know that money talks? Stop saying "yes ma'am" to mammon every time it calls you! Your manager says, "Work overtime this week." And you say, "Yes, mammon." The company offers you double time to work on a holiday and you say, "Yes, mammon." Then comes family trouble because you are never home.

"He that is greedy of gain troubleth his own house; but he that hateth gifts shall live." (Prov. 15:27)

"For the love of money is the root of all evil...." (1 Tim. 6:10)

"Evil" is "live" spelled backward. "Devil" is "lived" spelled backward. Which means "lived" spelled backward is death. Live or die; life or death. To serve mammon is a sin and the wages of sin is death. Stop working yourself to death over mammon!

Always be slow to spend. It takes faith to capture money and not spend it. Notice I said "capture" money and not "save." Saved money is for a different purpose than captured money. If I save money, eventually I am going to spend it. Captured money will be working for me from generation to generation. When I capture money, I immediately put it to work. This is a mystery revealed to me in Christ.

The Word of God says that the only fight we are supposed to be fighting is the good fight of faith. We are not supposed to be fighting the devil or anyone else. The devil is already defeated. Money is the god of this world, not satan. God says that you cannot serve both him and mammon (money). He did not say you cannot serve both God and satan. He said mammon! So people are serving money. Do not serve money. On the back of every US Federal Reserve Note it states, "In God we trust." Do not trust in the god of money.

The people who pay attention to money are the ones that do not have any. Money loves attention. It will chase after you for attention. Money wants you to think about the cares of this world, but God does not. The Lord God wants us to set our heart on things eternal, the things of heaven. The things of this world are going to pass away, but God's Word will stand forever. I am trying to encourage you to change your mindset about money. People are not broke because they do not have any money. They are working every day. People are broke because they do not have faith and it takes faith in God to be able to capture money and band it up. Of course, there are exceptions to everything and I realize that for some, the recession has been a time of hardship. However, the basic concepts don't change. The idea here is that we work for the almighty dollar when we should be focusing on the things of the kingdom of God.

I have been working for banks for over twenty-two years, so I know firsthand that people have difficulty saving money. I believe the problem is that Americans are consumer minded. We as a nation are mostly spenders. This is the reason why the credit system has been able to rule and reign in people's lives. Americans depends on the world's credit system as their source, not the Lord God.

God was Adam, Abraham, Isaac, Jacob, Job, Joshua, David, and Jesus' only source, not the Herod and Pharaoh's credit system. If you have credit cards, you have another source. You are saying to the Lord God that if he does not give it to you, you have another way to get it. Some people call their other sources credit cards, pawn shops, pay day shops, cash shops, Momma, Daddy, finance loan companies, banks, etc.

Jesus wants us to have faith in God. If you have faith in God, you will see the glory of the Lord revealed in your life. Personally, I just bind up the god of this world, mammon or money, by putting a rubber band around it. That way, it is in captivity until I let it loose. I have to loose it to spend it. Whatever I bind in heaven will be bound in earth. I set my mindset on heavenly things, not worldly things.

So I have bound up my worldly mindset and walked after the Spirit to heavenly places. Whenever you are walking after the flesh, you are walking in a worldly mindset. You are trying to impress people. Your spirit of money wants to be seen. Therefore, money is your god.

Whenever you are walking after the Spirit, you are walking in a kingdom mindset. You do not care about what people think of you. Kingdom citizens are not trying to impress others. They walk in love, peace, and joy. Your houses, cars, and clothes do not impress kingdom men and women. A kingdom man is in the God class. He is filthy rich and wealthy. He does not need anything. He has everything he needs because God is his source. So whatever you are toiling to have, God will give it to a kingdom man or woman and it will add no sorrow to his or her life.

Worldly-minded people are in debt and living in sorrow from most of the things that they have obtained through the world's system of credit. Instead of binding up the money, putting it in the corner of the bank somewhere, and daring it to move, worldly-minded people are stacking it up. They want to be seen in their fancy clothes and cars, but they are stacked up and racked up in debt.

Instead of letting the money put a band around me, I should be putting a band around the money. Instead of letting the world system work me, I need to work the system. Let's have a moment of silence as you process all of this...

BUBBLE GUTS

Jesus had the bubble guts on the cross. That is why he carried his paddle (cross): to bury that stinking stuff, called sin, in the ground. Back in the day, when men went to relieve themselves, they had to take a paddle with them, dig a hole in the ground, and cover up the dung. That stinking stuff had to be covered up. Well, all Christ did with the stench of sin was to bury it in the ground and he came out clean. Hallelujah! I know you all are thinking that I am playing around, but you should know me by now.

"Thou shalt have a place also without the camp, whither thou shall go forth abroad: And thou shalt have a paddle upon thy weapon; and it shall be, when thou wilt ease thyself abroad, thou shalt dig therewith, and shalt turn back and cover that which cometh from thee: For the Lord thy God walketh in the midst of thy camp, to deliver thee, and to give up thine enemies before thee; therefore shall thy camp be holy: that he see no unclean thing in thee, and turn away from thee." (Deut. 23:12-14)

FATHERLESS GENERATION

Many have no father figure. If God is not your father, then you do not have a father figure. A Fatherless home means that there might be a dad in the home, but God the Father is not the head of the household. He's also not the head of the dad in the home. Thus, the generation is Fatherless.

Since I have spiritually matured, I am not walking as a young son anymore. I am walking in the authority of the Father.

Men who don't work, don't eat. If you work, you will find a way to get food. Most men have a lack of ambition and no vision when it comes to future generations.

The Lord God gave me the keys to the kingdom. The nine fruits of the Spirit are the keys. This is the power that Jesus walked in. Against such, there is no law. My faith overrules the law. Amen, so be it.

MAGNIFY

The Lord will magnify those of us that are in Christ. He himself does not need to be magnified. He is already big. You are the one that needs to be magnified. To magnify means to make bigger and clearer so that you can see it better. I can use a magnifying glass to look at a small word on a piece of paper or a tiny ant on the ground. Why do I need to magnify someone who is already big enough to see with my natural eyes?

The Lord will magnify you. That is why you are so hot. The sun is shining on everyone, but the Lord God has his magnifying glass on you alone. And he has to be careful not to leave the magnifying glass on you too long; otherwise the sun is going to set you on fire. Hallelujah! The Lord is already magnified. He is trying to magnify you.

God will set you on fire like a poking iron. Have you ever left a poking iron in the fire too long and the poking iron catches fire? The poking iron is in the fire and the fire is in the poking iron. If you take that hot poking iron out of the fire and touch stubble or a piece of paper, it will set the stubble and the paper on fire. The poking iron will do it!

You are a poking iron and Christ is the fire. If I abide in him, then he abides in me. Let somebody come in contact with me if they want to. I will set them on fire!

EAGLE TALK

"Ye have seen what I did unto the Egyptians, and how I bare you on eagles' wings, and brought you unto myself."

(Exod. 19:4)

"Saul and Jonathan were lovely and pleasant in their lives, and in their death they were not divided: they were swifter than eagles, they were stronger than lions."

(2 Sam. 1:23)

"Behold, he shall come up as clouds, and his chariots shall be as a whirlwind: his horses are swifter than eagles.

Woe unto us! for we are spoiled."

(Jer. 4:13)

"Who satisfieth thy mouth with good things;

so that thy youth is renewed like the eagle's."

(Ps. 103:5)

"For wheresoever the carcase is, there will the eagles be gathered together."

(Matt. 24:28)

"…Wheresoever the body is, thither will the eagles be gathered together."

(Luke 17:37)

"For the Lord's portion is his people; Jacob is the lot of his inheritance. He found him in a desert land, and in the waste howling wilderness; he led him about, he instructed him; he kept him as the apple of his eye. As an eagles stir up her nest, flutter over her young, spread abroad her wings take them, bear them on her wings: So the Lord alone did lead him, and there was no strange god with him."

(Deut. 32:9-12)

BEWARE

"Beware not to be waxed fat, and kicked back with worldly fullness; Beware not to forsake God which made you who you are; Beware not to lightly esteem the Rock of your salvation; Beware not to provoke him to jealousy with strange gods with abominations and provoking him to anger by getting fat and growing thick when God is prospering you."

(Deut. 32:15-16)

JUBILEE

Jubilee is called the year of liberty:

"…where the Spirit of the Lord is, there is liberty (jubilee)."

(2 Cor. 3:17)

PROLOGUE

The purpose of graduating from church school was to let the Father know that I was willing to do good and to focus my heart, soul, and mind on him. The purpose of this book is to help people grow up in Christ. Anything that you wrap up in purpose, the Lord God says you can have. The Lord's purpose for our lives is to grow us spiritually from babes in Christ to mature Christians. He wants us to be doers of his Word, not just hearers.

The Lord God wants to have a personal relationship with each one of us. He is not satisfied with people just knowing who he is. He wants to make his abode in us; he wants to dwell in us: "…(he) hath broken down the middle wall of partition between us." (Eph. 2:14) He does not want us to be "…strangers and foreigners, but fellowcitizens with the saints, and of the household of God…." (Eph. 2:19)

The Lord God wanted to reconcile me back to the Father. Jesus came to save me and to get me back in the right relationship with the Father, just like Adam was before sin and the fall of man. In order to do this, I had to place my trust in the Lord. God's Word became my fuel. I took in his Word and used it for my fuel for godliness. To be like God is to be godly, because God is good. Jesus said, "Why callest thou me good? there is none good but one, that is, God." (Mark 10:18) The reason why goodness comes out of me is because

God is in me. My heart desires to dwell in the house of the Lord.

I thank you, Lord, for your grace and mercy. Thank you for seeing me right where I was and watching over me. I thank you, Lord, for leading me up higher. You brought me out of the valley; from hanging out amongst the tiny rocks to hanging out with the big rocks. On Christ, the solid rock, I now stand!

There isn't anything that the Father does not see. He is concerned about everything that happens. I have heard of people getting angry with God because of the death of a relative or close friend. I even got angry myself when those close to me died: my brother, grandparents, uncles, and college buddy. I wondered where God was then. But one day, I received the revelation of where God is when our loved ones die. He is in the same place where he was when his son died: on the throne.

God is on the throne watching over everything we do. No matter who you are, there are still gaps and breaches in your life that the enemy tries to attack in order to break your spirit. Know that the enemy cannot do anything to you without the Lord's approval. God has provided a way of escape from every situation. Storms come and go. When I got saved, I did not become exempt from the attacks of the enemy. As a believer, everything worked out for my good, bringing me closer to the Father. So I can count it all joy when I go through trials. Trouble does not last, meaning it will stop at some point. If you do not believe me, ask Job. Satan could not do anything to Job until God gave him permission. Even then, God told him what he could and couldn't do.

In the salvation walk, I have learned to be content in whatever state I am in; to be happy where I am. Although the enemy took away Job's money, family, and friends, he could not take Job's joy. The joy of the Lord is my strength. I am happy because the Lord is happy. I have learned contentment through my experiences and it is attainable only through the Holy Spirit, who teaches all things.

I challenge you to start thanking the Lord God right now for where you are in your spiritual walk. He wants you to be confident that you are heading in the right direction; he knows that you desire to grow up and mature spiritually in him. Continue studying to show yourself approved, continue to rightly divide the Word of Truth, and don't be afraid to step out in faith. I love you, my brothers and my sisters, and I pray that you will continue on in holiness and godliness.

THE END OF BOOK TWO...

www.ingramcontent.com/pod-product-compliance
Lightning Source LLC
Chambersburg PA
CBHW061653040426
42446CB00010B/1726